DOING
BUSINESS
BY THE
BOOK

DOING BUSINESS

BY THE

BOOK

HOW TO CRAFT A CROWD-PLEASING BOOK AND ATTRACT MORE CLIENTS
AND SPEAKING ENGAGEMENTS THAN YOU EVER THOUGHT POSSIBLE

SOPHFRONIA SCOTT

Published by Advantage, Charleston, South Carolina.
Member of Advantage Media Group.

ADVANTAGE is a registered trademark and the Advantage colophon is a trademark of Advantage Media Group, Inc.

Printed in the United States of America.

ISBN: 978-1-59932-093-9
LCCN: 2008938435

Most Advantage Media Group titles are available at special quantity discounts for bulk purchases for sales promotions, premiums, fundraising, and educational use. Special versions or book excerpts can also be created to fit specific needs.

For more information, please write: Special Markets, Advantage Media Group, P.O. Box 272, Charleston, SC 29402 or call 1.866.775.1696.

For Darryl

and

Tain Elijah

Table of Contents

Acknowledgments

A book never comes into the world all by itself. This book had many people who, directly or indirectly, contributed to its creation.

I would like to thank Baeth Davis and Fabienne Fredrickson, my mastermind mates who have encouraged and guided me through this wonderful growth period in my business. I thank Alexandria Brown, without whom this business would not have existed at all. I thank James Roche for a single idea that has made me a lot of money, Kendall Summerhawk for the inspiration I garnered from her book, *Brilliance Unbridled,* and my agent, Brettne Bloom, simply for just being there. I thank Heather Jackson for letting me know it was okay to do this one on my own, and Timothy Ferriss for being such an inspirational maverick. I thank Jack Canfield and Mark Victor Hansen for showing me what is possible with books. I thank Dan Kennedy, Bill Glazer, and Lee Milteer for showing me what is possible with entrepreneurship.

I thank my assistant, Andrea Davis-Powell, for her ongoing support. I thank the Cyrenius H. Booth Library in Newtown, Connecticut, where most of this book was written. I thank Adam Witty of Advantage Media for producing this book. I thank Meg Muckenhoupt for her humor and support in being a fellow mom who is always looking for time to write. Last but not least I thank all of my clients and workshop students who showed me that what I have to say has value. My gratitude knows no bounds.

Introduction

My business was born of my first book, and it wasn't even nonfiction. Two things happened that set me on the path to creating the **Done For You Writing & Publishing Company**. The first: I traveled around the country to promote my novel (*All I Need to Get By*, **St, Martin's Press**) and at every event I found myself answering more questions about how I got the book written and published than about the book itself. I didn't understand why: isn't this information out there everywhere? I finally decided it wasn't—at least not in a way that made it easy for people to put it to good use.

Then, the second event: a few months after my novel was published, I was nominated for a Best New Author award and attended a party with my fellow nominees. I enjoyed rubbing elbows with names I had only known before in print, so the afternoon was thrilling for me. At one point, though, I got into an intense conversation with another well-published author who was complaining about the number and poor quality of self-published books in the marketplace. "Just because you have a computer, that doesn't make you a writer," she said. She went on to point out that everyone may have a story, but that didn't mean it deserved to be published.

I listened to her—I probably even nodded my head once or twice! But for the rest of the evening and weeks afterward that conversation bothered me. I didn't know why until I finally realized that her comments struck at the heart of what I hold to be a deep personal belief: if people want to create, to bring something vital and new into the world, then they should be able to do it.

I look at it another way: everyone deserves to express himself or herself. Everyone deserves to deliver his or her message. I've found the groups that don't do that enough are speakers and small business owners. Every business is a creative endeavor. Every business is in some form an expression of the entrepreneur who made it. He or she put too much of themselves in it to be any other way. It shows up in the way the phone is answered, in how a customer is handled, in how a website is developed, in the quality of the product or service.

But in order for a business to go to the next level, the entrepreneur has to step out from behind the computer, counter, lectern, whatever, and put that message down on paper to reach out to a wider audience. There's never been a better time to do this because the marketing mavericks of our time (Dan Kennedy, T. Herv Eker, Jeffrey Gitomer) have totally refined the way a book can be used as a marketing tool. They did it right under our noses and in a way that has made them a lot of money. You'll see that I reference many of the same books again and again. That's because these strategies for how to effectively use a book to promote a business are still so new that only a handful of authors do them and do them really well.

How exactly did they do it? How did they change what goes into a book and how to sell a book? How did they revolutionize the publishing industry and make a published book the near equivalent of a business card?

Yes, I said business card. Just think of how important a business card is. Often it's the first thing an entrepreneur creates right after creating the business itself. And what happens if you go to a networking event and say, "Oh, I don't have a business card. I haven't made one yet." You just might get this response: "What! No business card? Are you crazy?"

We're now at that point with books: You don't have a book to your name? Are you crazy? Welcome to the new world of **creative commerce**!

I'm activating a grace period, and it goes into effect right this minute as you're reading this. For now you're not crazy—you just didn't know better. This book will take care of that. I will show you how a book can be the most powerful marketing tool your company has to its name. I'll also show you how to create that book so your target audience will know immediately that they must have that book, and that it will give them exactly what they're looking for. I'll break down the whole book-building process into easy chunks with my own organizational system that will make it so easy the book can practically write itself.

I know writing a book is usually seen as a process taking months, even years. But breaking things down into the essentials is what I'm trained to do. As a former magazine journalist, I spent fifteen years at *Time* magazine and *People* magazine gathering huge amounts of information week after week and boiling it down into two- and three-page magazine stories. This skill is particularly pertinent here because

1. You're a businessperson. Your time is important and you must learn things quickly.

2. You're a businessperson. Not having a book is costing you money! You have to fix this really fast.

And you will. The goal here is for you to be able to create effective books (Yes, that's plural. Why write just one?) that will bring you business, customers, and speaking engagements and put you and your business on the map.

Let's get started.

Part I:

WHY DO YOU NEED A BOOK?

You don't. Your business does! If you're a small business owner, speaker, coach, or consultant and you don't have a published book to your name, then you're missing an outrageously huge piece of your business. When you don't publish a book, when you don't take full advantage of the knowledge and experience that it has taken you years to accumulate, you are leaving a serious amount of money on the table. You're also missing the chance to make your business stand out in the marketplace against your many competitors.

Writing, publishing, and marketing a book can be a tremendous investment of time and money—and so many entrepreneurs have too little of both! That's why many aspiring authors won't embark on the journey until it's clear they will get something (preferably dollars) out of it. Trouble is, that's the same thinking that keeps them from ever doing a book. Entrepreneurs are all about the numbers and they don't know how to make money with a book beyond the traditional model of "sell book, get paid a royalty." Royalties can be slim pickings, sometimes just seven percent of the book's retail price. That's why entrepreneurs bypass doing a book unless they think they have the next *Good to Great* on their hands.

But thinking this way can actually **cost** you money! Without a book, you're missing out on

- attracting new and better quality customers.

- establishing your authority.

- quick and easy product sales.

How do you cash in? If you're looking to make more you'll have to think of your book as not just a book—you'll have to have a bigger picture in mind. That picture starts with you.

Chapter 1

STEPPING INTO THE SPOTLIGHT: YOUR MESSAGE, YOUR TIME

"Sophfronia's advice has helped me to re-think and re-focus my book idea, leading me closer and closer to the perfect vehicle to both promote my consulting business and to educate small business professionals on using the Internet to successfully market their businesses."

Joanne Marcinek
AskJoanne.com | Sandy Hook, CT

The best thing I can do for you and your book is happening right now. You might even feel it. It feels like someone knocking you in the side of your torso, a kind of pushing or prodding. Feel that? It's me and my sharp elbows, nudging you into the spotlight!

You might be thinking, "Oh, I'm not afraid to be in the spotlight. I'm in business or I'm a speaker after all!" I can understand that, but know this: being in the spotlight as an author is different. People will look at you differently because you've become a published author. It means more. Suddenly you're in print and can be held to everything you've written down.

You would think speakers step into the spotlight everyday and do it easily and naturally. They're out there in public all the time talking straight from the heart. But I have a sneaking suspicion that part of them thinks that once they've said their speech and it's out there, people will forget what they said. It makes them feel safe. They can lay it all out on the line and let it dissipate into the air. Putting it down in a book—well that's a different matter! My goodness, people could actually read it and pin them down for their views and what they said! That's just too scary!

I start the book process here by nudging you into the spotlight because I believe there are many feelings associated with the fear of just that that keeps aspiring authors from writing. When they don't write, that leads to an even bigger level of frustration and procrastination sets in. They get stuck.

I've known many high-achieving go-getters who get big stuff done every single day in their lives and in their businesses. But the one thing they can't do is get into a chair and finish writing their books. I recently listened to a group coaching call in which one of the participants was lamenting his inability to get excited about his work enough to finish it. Of course, that's not what he admitted when the session began. The work he talked about involved a million other things he thought were frustrating to him. He talked about grant proposals, fundraising programs, and all the other things he worked on. But when the coach delved deeper we discovered that what the guy was really upset about was the fact that he'd been working on a book for four years and couldn't finish it.

What's all the procrastination about?

Fear and Loathing in the Office

Some of the procrastination is about fear. It's a big thing to write down what you really believe. You constantly ask yourself, "What if someone doesn't like it? What if they say unkind things?"

Let's get over that right now. This may not be what you want to hear, but know this: **backlash is certain.** That goes doubly if you have a successful book on your hands. You'll discover there are people who want to criticize, point fingers, complain, or even be downright mean about what you wrote. Nine times out of ten, what they're doing or saying has nothing to do with you. If anything, it's about their own frustrations over not doing what you have done. The only way for them to make that hurt and frustration go away is to lash out at you and your work.

Timothy Ferriss learned this when his groundbreaking book *The 4-Hour Workweek* came out. Yes, he received tremendous praise and rave reviews. He also received many negative reviews, with people targeting him personally and using words like "hypocritical" and "shallow" to describe him and his freewheeling lifestyle. Mr. Ferriss travels the world dancing in tango competitions, participating in and winning marshal arts contests, and having a good time in general. I'm pretty sure some of the criticism aimed at this young, successful Princeton man comes from sheer envy over not being able to do all the fun stuff he does. Who is he to get to grab life by the horns like that?

That doesn't mean the criticism didn't hurt any less. Nobody wants to be called shallow. But Mr. Ferriss handled it well and even made it fruit for his blog postings. Would he not have written the book if he'd known beforehand about the coming backlash? I doubt it.

So backlash is certain. The real question is how will you take it when it happens? You have to be able to process it. Figure that out and then start writing. Here are a few tips to help you.

- **Delete and Conquer:** I've become quite adept at hitting the "delete" key whenever I find unkind e-mails in my inbox. The trashcan in your office works just as well if you get negative articles or letters in the mail. But you have to go deeper than just throwing the stuff away, especially if you're prone to take things personally. It doesn't work if you delete a message but keep reading it over and over in your head. You have to learn how to hit "delete" in your brain as well so the bad reaction to getting criticism doesn't fester.

- **The No-Fail Antidote:** You can neutralize the effects of negative messages by keeping a folder of all the great things people say about you. Fill it with testimonials from the people you've helped or even a running list of sales or requests for your service. Pick it up and read something from it immediately when you feel fear or doubt creeping up on you. Doing this will help you defuse bad feelings before they can become big bad mental blocks stopping you.

- **Prepare for the Inevitable:** Begin now to put yourself in a frame of mind in which you expect and even hope for backlash. Yes, I said hope for it! Hope for nice, big, sensational public backlash. That kind of stuff sells books. As they say, bad publicity is better than no publicity!

Another Fear, Another Reason

There are *millions* of books in print. Libraries are full, and stores like Books-A-Million seem to be overflowing. Every week there are new books coming on the market. When I worked at *People* magazine I used to sit next door to the book editor. He had a separate room on our floor where the books that came in were stored, and still his office was jam-packed with books. So many books! Do you ever think of all the books that are already out there and worry, "I don't have anything to say to add to the discussion"?

You're not alone. I recently consulted with a client who had been trying to write a book for months, but she kept stopping herself. She writes a very popular blog read by millions of people. In the blog she often features her interviews with experts she considers to be greater than herself. Many of them are also the authors of great books on the same subject she blogs about. She just kept thinking, "What can I say that they haven't said already?"

This is a major block for aspiring authors—and a valid one. You want your book to be absolutely new and creative. You want to write about things no one has thought to put on paper before. But here's a little secret for you: few books are truly that new and that creative.

I encourage you to go to the bookstore or your local library and pick out a topic in any nonfiction section. Let's take money as an example. There are tons of books on money management. If you look at a book by Jane Bryant Quinn or Suze Orman or Jim Cramer, you'll find a lot of the same basic information on saving, investing, mutual funds, retirement accounts, taxes, and the like. But you might prefer Jim Cramer to Suze Orman and vice versa. What's the difference, especially if the information is the same?

Let's look at the self-help arena. Books by Jack Canfield, Stephen Covey, Marianne Williamson, Martha Beck, and countless others talk about goal-setting, taking responsibility, clearing life's clutter, deciding what you want. But the way Stephen Covey presents it is very different from how Martha Beck talks about it. And Marianne Williamson doesn't write the way that Jack Canfield does.

What's different? Simply this: the individual and his or her unique voice. If you have confidence and passion for your material, that unique voice will come through in your book. You'll also touch the reader who prefers your voice. That person will choose you over another author again and again.

I pointed this out to my client. The millions of people subscribing to and reading her blog didn't read it for nothing. They could get this material in many other places, but they wanted to get it from her. Her voice was like no other. She offered hope. If she really wanted to write a book on her subject, my client just had to think simply and consider her book an extension of her blog.

Here's what she ended up doing. She found her voice by going back to the basics. She went over her past blog postings and figured out how her personality came through in each one. She also examined the process that she took her clients through when they came to her for help. When she looked at these two areas she realized she did do, say, and write things differently from what was already out there. These were was things she did all the time and had taken for granted. She found her original voice.

This thinking also made it easier for her to connect with how effective a book authored by her could be. She saw firsthand, every day, how her coaching helped her clients. If she were to write down her process in a book, she could help so many more! Now not only did she know what to say in her book, the book had purpose and vision. She had found the heart and soul of her book   and the confidence to write it. Her reward? A book deal with a major publisher.

Motivational Magic

The inner game going on inside your head can stop you from writing your book. But here's another secret: the inner game can help you finish it as well. Motivation is the magic pill. When people ask me, "How did you finish that book?" or, "How do I get organized and how do I stay focused?" this is my answer: **it's all about your motivation.** In other words, it's about *why* you're writing and what you hope to get out of it. What helps someone to finish is the *drive* to finish. If what you see at the end isn't enticing enough, no amount of prodding will get you to complete your work. You have to want to do it.

Writing a book while the rest of your life is merrily speeding on around you will be challenging and distracting. It can be also be tiring and stressful, and it can make you want to quit. Only your deep, interior motivation is what will push you over hurdle after hurdle.

By the way, I'm not talking about personal cheerleading or positive self-talk because, although those things are also necessary, their immediate effects last only a moment.

I'm talking about solid, long-term motivation that comes from 1) understanding yourself, and 2) understanding your work, which means knowing what you and others will get from your work.

Being motivated is about making a strong connection to your writing and your book, acknowledging that it is a part of you and your business. In order for you to reach your highest level, it's in your best interest to follow your path and complete this book. So how do you develop this kind of motivation?

Doing What You Value

Determining your values is indispensable for increasing and maintaining motivation. Why? Because your writing will reflect your values. If I were to ask you to tell me right now, what value is motivating you to write this book, your immediate answer might be money which would be absolutely fine. But I'm going to challenge you to go deeper than that. Because when the going gets tough—and it will—I'm willing to bet that money is not going to be motivating enough to get your book written.

It's also not enough to help you to write a book that people can relate to. Readers can see "shallow" coming from miles away. But, on the positive side, they can also see if you have some personal beliefs invested in your writing. When you express thoughts with passion, that kind of book is a beauty to behold, even if the reader doesn't agree with the thoughts of the author.

Marketing expert Dan Kennedy's books are called "No B.S." for a reason—that's what he believes and that's the way he lives. The guy takes No B.S.! He's fierce in his time management. He has rules for how and when he can be contacted, and his clients know they must adhere to them or get "fired." He attacks the rules of entrepreneurship and marketing in the same way. His readers pick up his books because they know he's shooting straight from the hip and that's what they want—no-nonsense advice that's going to be highly effective.

What would you want a reader to expect from a book of yours?

So, why are you writing your book? I know you want it to help your business, but ignore that one for a moment and think broader. Are you sharing a skill? Are you sharing new strategies? Are you going to help millions lose weight in a whole new way? Are you helping drug addicts transition to a world of recovery? Are you going to inspire a whole new generation of entrepreneurs?

What values are you expressing with these goals? By answering these questions you strengthen your connection to your writing and bolster your source of motivation. A lot of people don't think about what they value, but values are what drive us. We do what we do because of what we value.

Values are the behaviors that we are naturally attracted to. How do you behave when something is important to you? You don't hesitate, right? You take the steps you have to take and you do what needs to be done. Most times you don't even have to schedule what you need to do. You just do it!

Unfortunately we often don't take the time to think about our values until we are faced with a crisis such as a family member becoming ill or the loss of a job. Think about what happens and how you behave when your world starts falling apart. In a time of crisis your priorities become crystal clear and you act accordingly. You become intensely focused. You figure out how to do what needs to be done, often marshalling outside forces to help in the process.

But what happens in our everyday, non-crisis mode? Outside of emergencies we tend to be kind of fuzzy in terms of what's important or what to focus on. Making decisions when your values are fuzzy is difficult. It's hard to commit to and follow through on a goal such as finishing a book.

Take a moment to think deeply about what is important to you and what your values are. Afterwards you can create writing goals connected to them. When you think about your values, look at the question as if you *are* your values. If you value creativity, are you creative? If you value family connections, are you truly close to your family? If you value love, are you loved?

Remember, values are the behaviors that you're naturally inclined to, and often these will go all the way back to your childhood. I have always been interested in flowers. I tend to living things, and I like to help things grow. I've also been very creative since childhood. I loved to write and draw pictures based on what I read in books. Is it any wonder that, as an adult, I still garden and I still write? And you can see by my work that I still love helping people to grow. So anyone can see upon examining my life that my values are creativity, teaching, inspiring others, and being connected.

The times in my life when I've been dissatisfied always reflected the fact that I was not living my values; in those times I felt limited and I felt frustrated. If I had taken on a big project or tried to write my book when I was in an unfocused time, I would not have succeeded because, most likely, what I would be pushing to do would not have been connected to anything important to me.

In fact, I did try to write a book proposal at a time when I was very dissatisfied and unfocused. It was for a nonfiction book on a subject that I knew little about. Every word I wrote for that book proposal was a struggle, and there was no way I would have succeeded in completing the book. It was not connected to who I was.

But you can succeed in writing for your business. It will be the right goal if you start right here and identify your key values. Think of it as a golden opportunity: maybe in the rest of your life you don't get to express your values as clearly and directly as you would in writing a book.

If You Need Help...

If you'd like some guidance in clarifying your values we have an excellent values assessment on our Web site. Just go to www.DoneForYou-Writing.com/values.html to download your copy.

CHAPTER 2

LEADING EXPERT LAND:
THE FAST TRACK TO AUTHORITY

"I have never been this clear about my message or what I do. Working with Done For You has helped me focus and now I talk with people about my theories and systems with total confidence. I am more effective because of my clarity. I'm even getting a radio show—that's how much I've changed! I could never have done that before. In the past I would have rambled on and confused people. Now my message is crystal clear, and my book and my voice deliver it to my audience."

Thomas Milligan IV
Milligan Mortgage, LLC | Newtown, CT | www.MilliganMortgage.com

When I was in college I spent a good amount of time being in awe of the people around me. I was at Harvard, after all, and my teachers and fellow students were all super smart and doing amazing things like writing operas, exploring new theories of economics, and explaining society through the study of ants. I was impressed and assumed everyone knew more than I did about everything.

In my sophomore year, following through on my love of the theater, I took on the job of assistant stage manager for a large production of two of Sam Shepard's one-act plays, "Suicide in B-Flat" and "Action." The director was one of the prominent names in American Theater; the actors, especially the seniors, were the best on campus—

one was Amy Brenneman who went on to star in the popular television series, *Judging Amy*.

One night in rehearsal for "Action," the actors were practicing a scene in which a guy comes in with a bucket of water, pulls a fish out of the bucket, and proceeds to clean the fish onstage. That night was the first night they were using a real fish.

The actor pulled the fish out, threw it on the table, and then paused. The whole scene stopped and I didn't understand why. Finally the director stood up: "Okay, does anyone here know how to clean a fish?"

I looked around the quiet room, stunned because no one answered him. I had grown up near the shores of Lake Erie and my father had fed our large family by catching or buying lots of fish. I would sit in the backyard with my siblings cleaning all of it and by the age of eleven I had a pretty thorough familiarity with the guts of several kinds of fish.

I held up my hand and said, "I do." People stepped aside and made way for me as I went to the stage. I showed the actor how to hold the knife and how to hold the fish. I informed the prop master on what kind of fish to buy for the run of the show since the kind we had there was too spiny—the actor could cut himself on the fish. Everyone listened. I was the authority.

That was my first experience in having authority, and as I've gotten older I understand it more and more. Here are two important points I've come to believe as true with authority:

1. People are quite willing to give way to someone who knows more than they do. At first I understood this only to mean they listen to you, but it's more than that. It also means

they're willing to trust you, give you responsibility, and **give you money** if they perceive your authority.

2. You don't have to know that much more than the other person to be considered an expert. As they say, in the land of the blind, the one-eyed man is king. When you think about it, with a little self-study you can become an expert in anything fairly quickly.

I learned this when I started out my career as a researcher at *Time* magazine. Week after week I had to become a quick expert in many different topics from aircraft carriers to mergers and acquisitions to the Mormon Church. The work usually involved a huge amount of reading in a short period of time. But I did it and did it well enough to spot mistakes in the written story before it went to press.

We all become quick experts everyday. Usually we do it when misfortune strikes, and then we're learning all we can about a disease or how to fix something in our home. But we also become experts when we research our vacations, pregnancies, diets, or cars.

If you can do this and be perceived as an expert and impress guests at dinner parties, just think of how effective you can be putting all the expertise of your profession on paper in a book.

One of the ways the dictionary defines *authority* is "the power to influence others, especially because of one's commanding manner or one's recognized knowledge about something." I should also point out that "authority" and "author" have the same origins—so they naturally go hand in hand!

Authors are still considered **very special people** in our society. We mutually acknowledge that writing a book is a pretty tough thing to do, so when someone actually does it, we are all impressed by it. We know it takes gumption to follow through. If that guy made himself sit down and write two hundred to three hundred pages, then it stands to reason that he must have something important to say. He made a commitment to the project; he invested the time necessary to put his message down on paper. Folks who believe they themselves lack that kind of commitment are truly impressed with someone who does. They happily cede the upper hand to you.

What does this mean for you? **Instant authority!** That means:

- Potential customers will sit up and take notice because you literally "wrote the book" on the problem they're dealing with.

- Event organizers will want to invite you for speaking engagements (where you can sell even more copies of your book!).

- Other people in your field will you seek you out for consultations. (Make sure you charge them when they show up!)

Who do you think of when you want to read about marketing? Maybe Jay Conrad Levinson, Dan Kennedy, or Michael Port. What about money? T. Herv Eker or perhaps Loral Langemeier. Leadership? Gotta have Stephen Covey or John C. Maxwell. You may have even thought about their book titles before their names. That's authority. Even if you don't know these people before you pick up their books, you automatically assume they know what they're talking about because you're holding their book in your hands. That's pretty powerful.

How Your Book Fits In

Why does a book work so well to help establish your authority? To answer this, let's take a closer look at the mechanics of authority.

Gaining Your Expertise

You gain your expertise in one of two ways: doing a thing or studying it. I'm an expert in cleaning fish because I've done it. I'm an expert in writing and publishing books because I've done it. My clients are experts in marketing, motivation, cooking, feng shui, and dealing with credit because this is what they do in their businesses every day.

I can also say I'm something of an expert in the Beatles, cooking, potty training, gardening, yoga, and road cycling because I've done or studied all of these things.

Having the expertise is important—you have to be able to walk your talk and pony up the goods when the opportunity presents itself. But here's the rub: **the opportunity comes from how you make your expertise known.**

Wielding Your Expertise

You see, having authority is kind of a double-edged sword. People like to defer to people who have it, but if you're perceived as a know-it-all who can't or isn't willing to share or teach for the benefit of others, then people (and by that I mean customers or clients) aren't interested in being around you.

Former Vice President Al Gore is a perfect example. During his ill-fated run for the White House in 2000, he took a lot of flack in the debates for coming off as smug and condescending. Fast forward to 2006-2007, and now Mr. Gore is putting his brains to use for the good of our environment. He filmed *An Inconvenient Truth* and suddenly people started seeing him as the kindly yet kingly professor who was compassionately letting us know we were headed for a world of trouble with the global warming stuff. They were begging him to run for president again!

How can you demonstrate that you are willing to teach and share your expertise? With a book! When you craft a book, as you'll learn later in this one, you seek to solve a big problem for the reader. You instantly start from a position of wanting to help, and that's the first place where the reader will connect with you.

You start out by clearly outlining the problem and how it may be negatively affecting the reader. You let him or her know you have experience with the problem either from your own life or working with your clients. Then lay out your solution in whatever way you see as the best.

Don't worry if it seems like you're giving it all away. When people have a good experience they usually want more. In your case, they may want to hire you or come to a workshop so they can meet you in person. In fact some authors, like Dan Kennedy, encourage this by giving away free seminar tickets in their books.

What to Do With That Power

Even if you're not an entrepreneur, you can still earn financial benefits from your book. Think of it like this: **your book becomes your business**. You use it to attract speaking engagements, teaching gigs, or even consulting work. You could develop a high fee workshop or intensive around your book. Many of the teachers in continuing education programs such as those offered through The Learning Annex (www.learningannex.com) are authors who have done just that. If you're in the corporate world, think of this: few people get to walk around with the word "author" on their resume, so it's sure to stand out when you're hunting for your next job. In fact, it may bring you better offers!

With authority, you can also attract publicity, especially if your topic is tied to current events. Have you ever noticed that the guests interviewed on news programs are often introduced as "the author of such and such book"? Six times out of ten, the book is not one you'd find on the *New York Times* bestseller list. But is the quality of the exposure the person receives the same? You bet! You can get that same exposure for your business, too!

Part II:

WHAT TO DO WITH YOUR BOOK

Let's talk strategy. I put strategy before writing and there's a powerful reason why. You'll be more likely to finish your book—and do it quickly—if you have a clear plan for what you're going to do with it. I've heard so many entrepreneurs say, "I can't work on my book. I need to work on stuff that's going to bring me money right now. I have to pay the bills." I totally understand that. But this kind of thinking keeps you stuck in a survivor mode. You spend all your time trying to scrape together enough business just to get by and you never get around to doing the things that will skyrocket you to the next level. It becomes a never-ending loop.

Your book can bring in business quickly if you plan a strategy that will make it do so. Here's exactly how to do it.

CHAPTER 3

THE PURPOSE OF YOUR BOOK

"Sophfronia taught me so much about the writing process, both in how to shape a good proposal as well as how to come up with a good structure and content for a book. Greatly due to her guidance, I pitched a nonfiction book to a major publisher and got a five-figure advance in a competitive market."

Pamela Slim

Mesa, AZ | Author of the Blog, "Escape From Cubicle Nation", www.EscapeFromCubicleNation.com

I read a lot of articles about writers and the things they have to say about the publishing process. Some of them are disappointed in the process. Usually, it's because they had certain expectations that were not met. Whether they knew it or not, there was no way those expectations were going to be met because of the way they chose to have their books published. It seems to me that the way to avoid that kind of disappointment is to be clear about what you want and to make sure that you're pursuing an avenue that will get those needs met.

For instance, if making a lot of money is your reason for writing a book, understand that it's going to be hard for a first time author to do that through a traditional publisher. Normally, as a first time author, you don't have a very big following. Consequently, you're not going to get a big advance, and the royalty package is usually not a lot of money. If to make a lot of money is truly your goal, you would be better off self-publishing your book and then launching a big marketing push to sell as many copies as you can. That way, you get to keep more of the profit for yourself versus having to share it with a zillion other people, as you will in the traditional publishing route.

In the same vein, if you have a different desired outcome, for example if you are thinking of yourself more as a famous author on the *New York Times* bestseller list and the money you make really isn't an issue, you might want the prestige that comes from being with a major publishing house like a Penguin, Random House, or Harper Collins. If that is the goal you're working on, self-publishing wouldn't be an option. You're going to be focused on doing all the things you need to do to get the attention of a traditional publisher, whether that be

- developing a following

- taking lots and lots of writing courses to improve your work

- looking for an agent to represent you to get you into a bigger publishing house.

You also have to remember that your experience may be a little different because your book will be very connected to your business. Here are three things to keep in mind.

1. Don't get caught up in the numbers in terms of thinking whether or not you have a "bestseller." In the publishing world, selling five thousand copies as a first time author can be considered a success, but it could be meaningless to your business if you didn't generate five thousand leads or five thousand more sales of other products. Get in the habit of looking at the numbers from the viewpoint of your business. How many clients did the book bring in this month? How many speaking engagements? You get the idea.

2. Size does matter. You might believe a book isn't really a book if it isn't at least three hundred pages, but will your target

audience read a book of that length? Some audiences will and some won't. It's your job to figure out what yours wants. It's not good to produce a slim, one-hundred-page volume if your readers think heft equals seriousness. Likewise you don't want to write a dictionary-size tome if your readers prefer simple strategies they can toss in a bag and take with them.

3. Hardcover or soft? Again, think about what your audience looks for. Many financial books come out in hardcover first. Softcover, of course, is less expensive to produce and more acceptable to a mass audience. I find it interesting that *The 7 Habits of Highly Effective People* has been available in softcover for years, but the cover most people think of is the royal blue one from the hardcover edition. Just something to consider...

How to Get Clear on Your Outcome

To get clear about your desired outcome, you have to create what I call a "publishing plan." To make a publishing plan, you ask yourself a series of questions and write the answers down so you can get a concrete picture of what you want.

Your Publishing Plan

1. The first thing you pose to yourself is a fill-in-the-blank statement: *I want my book to be* _____. Here you must ask yourself, do I want my book to be a product I'm going to sell when I get speaking engagements? Do I want it to be a door opener? Do I want it to be a gift that people are going to pass around? Do I want it to be a giant business

card? What exactly do you want your book to be, or to do, for you?

2. What do you want financially? Is it that you want a publisher to give you a huge advance, or you don't really care about the money? Be honest with yourself. What exactly do you want to happen financially with this book?

3. How long will you try to find a publisher without success before you decide to self-publish?

4. Who will buy your book? Who is your market?

5. What's your budget? How much are you willing to spend? (because even if you do have a traditional publisher, you're going to have to spend a certain amount of your own money to market and publicize the book).

6. How much of your effort, blood, sweat, and money are you willing to put into it? What are you willing to do to find the right agent and publisher? Are you willing to send out two hundred query letters? Are willing to spend money to go to conferences and try to meet people? Are you willing to spend the money to fly to New York City where you can knock on doors and try to meet people face to face?

7. How many books do you want in print? If you're going with a traditional publisher, you're not going to have any say in the matter. They make a decision, and that's the print run. If you self-publish, then you have an option to go with a company who can print up copies as you need them. Or maybe it's your goal to have ten thousand books in print and come hell or high water, you're going to put those books out into the world, sell them, or distribute them.

8. You also have to ask yourself about sales, even if you do get signed with a big publisher. Are you comfortable selling?

I used to think that the reason I went with a traditional publisher for my first book was so that I didn't have to sell my own book. I didn't want to have to cart around suitcases of my book. But I realized that channel is actually one of the ways that people do get books, and its acceptability is on the rise. So even though my first book was in stores and on Amazon, I still take my book around on my travels and sell it.

9. Next, you have to consider, especially if you're self-publishing, how you're going to get distribution. Are you going to be able to get a book to the places where it needs to be sold? What will it take for you to do that? Again, how many doors are you going to knock on? How much are you willing to pay? Are you willing to visit stores across the country to get it there?

10. The avenues through which you decide to publish your book will entail working with others on audience, marketing, distribution, and sales. Those people are part of your team. So, who will be on your team? Are you going to be doing this on your own (besides whatever printer you hire)? Are you going to have an editor on your team? Are you going to hire a designer? Are you going to hire a publicist?

If you answer all of these questions clearly and honestly you will have a comprehensive plan for how your book is going to make its debut in the world.

The whole book publishing process becomes easier when you have a clear plan, stick to it, and find avenues through which you can operate effectively. It also helps you to make decisions when new opportunities arise. Maybe someone will come to you saying, "Hey, I can put your book in a Crate & Barrel store." You can say, "Well, that would be nice, but that's not my target audience. My target audience shops at Urban Outfitters." Just the fact that you can answer that question indicates you have done your research and will make the most effective choices for the distribution of your book. A lot of writers would just be happy to have it in a store—but then what if the book doesn't sell? Well, why hasn't it sold? Because your target audience doesn't shop at Crate & Barrel.

The Myths of Publishing

You may be surprised when I say thatour goals will most likely send you to self-publish instead of going the route of finding a traditional publishing house. I don't say this to discourage you or to be negative. In fact, you can find information on the details of traditional publishing, which involve finding an agent, writing a book proposal and writing a query letter to entice potential editors and/or agents to your project, in a bonus chapter at the end of this book. But most new writers don't understand how difficult it is to attract a publishing house or what they need to do to improve their chances. I believe they are laboring under certain myths that make them believe they only need to be persistent to get past the flurry of rejection letters. I will go into these myths surrounding traditionally publishing since they'll help you see why you can get published quicker on your own.

One of the biggest myths I find new writers harbor is that somehow they're going to get a six-figure advance for their book. I'm not saying that's impossible, but certain things have to be in line for you to get a six figure advance. You're not just going to come out of the blue as an unknown author and get that much money unless you have something truly compelling to offer in terms of either your work itself or your platform.

What's platform? It's your ability to reach a certain audience. If you host a radio show, that could be considered part of your platform. The same goes for a television show, blog, newsletter, or calendar of speaking engagements. *Platform* is the big buzzword in the publishing business. When a publishing house buys your book, nine times out of ten, they're really buying your platform.

I know of one sample book proposal that recently did get a six-figure advance—but the authors of that book had a tremendous platform. They have a Web site that gets one hundred thousand hits a day. They are regularly interviewed in the top women's magazines like *Cosmopolitan*, *Working Mother*, and *Redbook*. These women are known in their field and have become the commanders of an ongoing conversation about women business owners. They were already bringing a huge audience to the table, and they were going to be able to sell a ton of books just because they announced their book's debut on their Web site. Unless you already have that kind of following already, though, don't go out thinking you're just going to get a huge check right away because you'll be sorely disappointed.

Another myth is that people think this money shows up all at once. The fact is that the publishing house will hold back as much money as it can. Even if you did get an advance of, let's say ten thousand dollars, you won't get it all at once. You'll get a portion of it, maybe half, when you sign the contract. You won't get the rest until you finish the book. The money gets doled out piecemeal. Even if you do earn royalties, they're only going to come in on a quarterly basis, and you won't even start getting anything like that until at least a year after the book has come out. So, this industry is usually not the place for writers to make fast money.

Returns are also an issue. Just because a bookstore has your book it doesn't mean it's a done sale. If they haven't sold a certain number of copies within a certain amount of time, the bookstore can send the book back to the publisher unsold. These can be taken off your count of books sold. That's why it takes so long for you to get money, because even the book publisher is not quite sure how many books have sold until they get the returns.

People might also assume that bigger is better, accepting the idea that everything is going to be great because Random House or Harper Collins is publishing the book. That's not necessarily so; you might not be getting the attention your book needs at a bigger publishing house. They may not have previous experience with your type of material, or the editor who was really into your material has suddenly moved on. People move around a lot in the publishing industry, especially at some of the big houses.

Don't give a publishing house that may be unknown to you short shrift. They may be more likely to put more money behind your book just because yours is one of only a few books they're putting out that year. Sometimes a small publisher has more incentive to promote you than a large publisher.

Then there's also the idea that the publishers know everything. Somehow, you are going to be validated if an agent or a publisher has chosen your book. That's a nice thing to have happen, but keep in mind that these are not gods. They can be wrong. You can get a book accepted, and then by the time you hand it in they've decided it doesn't feel timely anymore. They might decide either not to publish your book or to put it out there with no support at all. What kind of validation is that?

Be Proactive

Think of it this way. You wouldn't hand over control of your business to just anyone, would you? I would like for writers to be empowered about this process, to see that every step of the way they have choices, that they can be in charge of the outcome, and that the best thing is to not to hand over control to somebody else. I don't just mean control of the book; I mean control of whether or not you feel it was a success.

You have certain decisions that you've made about what you want. So if someone says, "Oh, this was horrible, it only sold five thousand copies," well, then you don't have to listen to that person, because you are doing what you want to do with your book and your business. I just want you to know you can take charge of the process. It's great if you can get with a big publishing house and it's great to get an agent, but it doesn't mean you hang up your brain.

CHAPTER 4

YOUR BOOK AS THE ULTIMATE
LEAD GENERATION TOOL

"I'm excited about the new material Sophfronia helped me develop, and even better, my clients LOVE it. It so fits my message and there's no way I could have come up with it on my own. I'm gonna have a big year thanks to my new book and my new system."

Steve Gavatorta

www.Gavatorta.com | Tampa, FL

What's the purpose of writing a book without giving the reader a way to connect with you? That's like writing down the secrets of the universe, not signing your name, putting the message in a bottle, and throwing it into the ocean! It's going to be pretty hard for the person who finds it to come back to you.

You may ask why having a person come back to you is so important, but as a businessperson I'm sure you already know what I'm talking about. In fact you probably spend a lot of money and time over it: **lead generation.**

What Exactly is Lead Generation?

Lead generation is all about mining the sea of people for the gold of your future prospects. You're looking for leads whenever you place ads, do cold calling, or collect names after a speaking engagement. Here we'll talk about seeking leads through your book. This concept is relatively new. In the old times of the traditional publishing world, a book would get sold and that was it. The author had no way of knowing who had bought it or where it went.

But in recent years the use of books as lead generation tools has been revolutionized by entrepreneurs such as Dan Kennedy, T. Herv Eker, and Jeffrey Gitomer. They've done it by putting stuff in books that most publishers would cringe at before. They include enticing offers and powerful **calls to action**.

What Exactly is a Call to Action?

A call to action is when you ask, order, and inspire your readers to take action. Preferably, that action would be to call, fax, or e-mail you to hire you or purchase products. At the very least you want them to give you their contact information.

What Makes a Great Call to Action?

What if you gave a call to action that required people to do more? What would make them do it? Go back and look at your favorite books that feature special offers, coupons, or requests. Which ones did you jump on? Why? Are they tools your market would connect with as well? Let's dissect a few popular books and see how they work.

Timothy Ferris's *The 4-Hour Workweek* features many subtle and not-so-subtle suggestions that you go to his Web site, where you have to give up your e-mail address to have access to the goodies he has in store for you. You can get help figuring out your "Target Daily Income" ("Online calculators on our companion site do all the work for you and make this step a cinch," Mr. Ferris writes) or you can get templates for email responses. But Mr. Ferris totally releases the mother lode at the end when he declares, "This book is not just what you hold in your hands." He then reveals there is more that couldn't fit into the book and that you can use "passwords hidden in this book" to access these extra materials. Of course you have to go to the Web site. Of course it's really juicy stuff he's offering up. The list includes:

- "How to Get $700,000 of Advertising for $10,000" (includes real scripts)

- "How to Learn Any Language in 3 Months"

- "Muse Math: Predicting the Revenue of Any Product"

- "Licensing: From Tae Bo to Teddy Ruxpin"

- "Online Round-the-World (RTW) Trip Planner"

Mr. Ferris tops it off with "For this and much more reader-only content, visit our companion site and free how-to message boards at www.fourhourworkweek.com. How would you like a free trip around the world? Join us and see how simple it is." How can you not respond to that? You can bet Mr. Ferris now has a mega mailing list and will be selling his strategies to this list for years to come.

Jeffrey Gitomer peppers his books with his wonderful "Free Git Bits," which call readers throughout his book to go to his Web site for goodies. But if you're a first time visitor to the site, you have to register to get the goods. In his *Little Black Book of Connections* the bits include:

- examples of how to give a free personal commercial

- bits you need to know about others to connect on a more personal level and build a relationship

- information on building your own e-zine

- a list of the 21.5 best places to network

- strategies and examples of personal commercial engagement.

Mr. Ferriss and Mr. Gitomer are really just refining methods already used by the big guns in business. Marketing guru Dan Kennedy recently published not one, but two books: *No B.S. Direct Marketing* and *No B.S. Wealth Attraction for Entrepreneurs.* The covers of both books (front and back) highlight the following offers:

- free audio CD inside the book

- free email course and direct marketing tool kit

- free $995 value seminar tickets

- free teleseminar invitation

- free newsletters

- the chance to enter a contest to win a Ford Mustang car.

Let's look at one more, *Secrets of the Millionaire Mind.* The author, T. Harv Eker, doesn't waste any time. The very first page of his book is a fancy looking graphic labeled "MILLIONAIRE MIND COURSE CERTIFICATE." It goes on to say, "T. Harv Eker and Peak Potentials Training invite you and one family member to attend the Millionaire Mind Intensive Seminar, as complimentary guests. To register and for more information…" Mr. Eker then directs you to a Web site as well as a toll-free phone number in case you don't have access to a computer. The certificate notes you have to provide a reference number or similar proof that you purchased the book.

Inside the book Mr. Eker again sends readers to the book's Web site for "FREE BOOK BONUSES" including "a free list of all the declarations in this book presented in calligraphy, in a printable format, suitable for framing." You can also subscribe, by providing your contact information of course, to the Millionaire Mind "thought of the week." He ends the book with a detailed description of each of his seminar programs and repeats the certificate graphic with the invention to attend one. He also pitches his "Home Learning Programs," basically the seminars made available on CD.

To me it looks like Mr. Eker's strategy is to get readers to show up in person so they can eventually purchase more seminars. If they're not ready for that, he can get their contact information and market to them until they are.

Now let's compare this with an old guard approach. The book is still popular and hugely successful: *The E-Myth Revisited* by Michael E. Gerber. He mentions in the book that his company, E-Myth Worldwide, teaches the strategies he's discussing in the book. Mr. Gerber even gives a tiny hint that he's holding back a little on the information because he wants you to contact the company to learn more.

Then, on the very last page of the book, is a form to fill out that you can fax or mail to E-Myth Worldwide to request more coaching. There's no offer of juicy freebies, no enticement other than your wanting to "take the first step." But what if you aren't ready for that first step yet? It's too easy for the lead to get away. There's no "in-between" access point made apparent for the person who wants to stay in contact until they are ready. Very old school.

Putting lead generation pages or information in your book won't cost you anything extra. In fact, you should place them throughout your book, not just at the end. It's sad to say it, but readers may not finish reading your book.

In fact, the funds will flow when you turn this new customer into a *purchaser* of your higher end products. And that task may be easier to do because, chances are, this will be a higher quality customer: this person has sought out your book, either online or in a bookstore. He has already paid for your knowledge, so you know he values what you have to say. If he is buying books, he is probably gathering information and will want more. Who better to give it to him than you?

Let's look at these add-ons and what they offer.

Variety

Everyone has different tastes and we all learn differently. Likewise one free offer may not be suitable for everyone. For instance, an invitation to a free seminar in Los Angeles is great, but if you're a working mother living in Charlotte, North Carolina, it may be difficult to accept. If you're picking up the author's book for the first time and just getting familiar with his or her work, you also don't have the motivation to make the effort—at least not yet. If this is the only offer in the book, the author can consider this valuable lead lost.

But if the reader can get two free months in the author's membership group and participate in the regular calls that are one of the benefits of membership, then our reader can easily sign up for that call or the recording of it without any resistance.

Let's go a step further. What if the reader doesn't want to commit to a phone call? Maybe he or she isn't comfortable being on the line with strangers, especially when it's a longstanding group. For this person you can offer a free CD. All they have to do is go to your Web site, enter a name and address, and it will get shipped right out. See how variety can benefit you? You're casting with a wider net and bringing in lots of leads, even the ones that almost got away!

Targeting Your Audience by Targeting Your Offers

Here's a more advanced way for you to work with variety in your offers: **you can tailor the offer to the kind of customer/client you wish to attract.** For instance, let's say you want a client who is proactive and willing to take steps on her own. This is very much a do-it-yourself type of client who really likes tools to help her do what she wants to get done. Therefore your offers throughout your book should send your prospective client to your Web site for a series of tools or assessments.

If you want clients who don't like to do things on their own because you want them to buy your help again and again, then you'll want to focus on your expertise and your personality. Your free offers will give prospects the opportunity to experience you as a live, exciting person. You'll want to pitch the free teleseminars, the free live seminars, and the audio CDs where they'll get to hear your voice. You'll also get to tell them over and over again that you have their solution and will help them with the problem they want you to solve.

Value

People like to get something for nothing. They don't like to get something for nothing if the something is junk. That's just the way we are: we don't want our cheap stuff to be cheap! That just means that when you make your offer you want to attach a value to it. There are three ways to do it:

1. **Perceived Value**: This involves how your client or customer perceives the value of what you're offering. Your job is to offer

a free tool that works, period. Then your prospects have to be able to see immediately how the offer can help them. You can't assign a specific dollar value because it will be different for each person. If the tool in question frees up time and the person believes his or her time is worth $150 an hour, then that's what that tool will be worth to that person. If a dentist sees how the tool can bring him one extra patient each month, then the value of that client is the value of the tool for that dentist.

2. **Value in Dollars**: You assign a dollar value to the offer. For instance, Dan Kennedy notes that he's offering a free seminar that the rest of the Joe Shmoe Public will have to pay $995 per ticket. He also gives away three free months in his Gold Inner Circle Membership. The price is listed at $39.97 per month, so automatically you know this offer is worth $119.91. The great thing about these offers—and you should remember this—is that this is not a random dollar amount pasted on the thing. Somewhere someone is actually paying these amounts, which makes the offer that much more attractive to the prospect. They get that added edge of feeling they're one up on somebody!

3. **Value in Dollars Saved:** In this instance you give something away that will help the reader save money. A perfect example of this is Timothy Ferriss's offer I mentioned that he will tell you how to get seven hundred thousand dollars worth of advertising for ten thousand. He targets the frugal mindset of his prospects and it pays off!

One warning: be selective in the number of offers you put in your book. You don't want too few, but you don't want too many either. Here's why: when you offer too much free or discounted stuff it lowers the perceived value in the whole package. If you keep adding on and adding on, after a while it just feels like clutter. You also risk overwhelming your prospect. Remember the old saying: "A confused mind says no." Same goes for the overwhelmed one.

An Invitation to Come Inside

What happens when someone puts up a sign that says "club" or "members only"? It makes you want to go inside, right? That's just a general rule even if the club has a silly name like Alfalfa's "He-Man Woman Haters Club" in *The Little Rascals*!

This gives you a unique opportunity to make an offer your prospect can't refuse: an offer to join your "elite" or "exclusive" or "gold" group membership program. This is simple to do. You give a short list of the benefits members will experience such as group calls, free audio, monthly call-in times with you, and anything else you have in the plan. Then you offer two to three months in the group free (you can charge minor—less than ten dollars—shipping or set-up charges if they apply). Then—and you make this *very clear*—you begin charging the person's credit card for their membership when the trial period is over.

Personal Access to You

Once you become an author everyone will want personal access to you. This could be counterproductive if your goal is to step back and have less one-on-one interaction with customers and clients. On the other hand it could be extremely productive—and profitable—if you can figure out how to charge them when they show up.

For instance, if you are a speaker skilled at selling from the stage, then your goal would be to invite as many prospects as possible to free live seminars. The idea is that you know you can get them into the back of the room to buy your product when you're done talking.

If you don't work with private clients anymore, you can make that clear to people who want to work with you. Then, if they insist you take them on you can always charge a huge fee. If they don't want to pay it, they'll go away and you'll be fine. If they do, you'll make a nice chunk of change and you'll be fine.

The point is to make decisions early on about your personal time, how you want to spend it, and how you value it. Then you can parse it out and charge accordingly.

How You Can Create Your Most Effective Call to Action

You'll know the results of your call to action when your list grows or your sales increase. But how exactly do you create an effective call to action? A great call to action has three aspects:

It's a no-brainer—you feel as though you must do it! This will follow from your material. If the reader is engaged with your methods and following your lead, then responding to a call to action will be a matter of course, another step or part of the program. For example, if you're following Timothy Ferriss's suggestion to figure out how much money you'll need to earn to take two months off, it's practically a no-brainer that you'll go to his Web site to use the calculator to help you do so.

It's irresistible—and free. We all like to get things for free, even more so when the thing being offered has tremendous value. The offer of a free seminar from Dan Kennedy is one thing. The fact that it's a seminar that he charges $995 for is the part that turns your head—and makes the offer irresistible.

It's easy. You don't want your prospect to have to jump through too many hoops to take advantage of your offer. You'll also want it to be very clear how to take advantage of the offer; explain what to do in detail. (Tell prospects to go to the site and enter their e-mail addresses, for instance.) Of course it can't be too easy—you don't want to attract a bunch of tire-kickers who will never become customers or clients. But a truly qualified prospect will appreciate the ease with which she can get something, especially if you provide good content and value in the process.

Plotting a Lead Generation Strategy

Your business will get the most bang from your book if you design a strong lead generation strategy in your book. There are many things to consider, but stay with me here. You'll find that every moment you spend setting your book up correctly to bring in good prospects will pay off down the road.

A strong lead generation strategy will do three things:

1.) **Qualify Prospects:** You don't want just anyone coming to you. You want potential ideal clients—people you'll enjoy working with, who respect your expertise and have no qualms about paying you what you're worth. You can qualify prospects with...

Your material—If you've followed the writing steps in this book really well, then the material in your book will automatically appeal to the people you want as ideal clients.

Your questions—You'll want to continually ask questions in your book to make the reader qualify himself. "Do you want do this?" "Is this you?" "Is this what you want?" Ideally you want the person to answer "Yes!" and raise his hand by going to your Web site or contacting you by mail, fax, or phone.

Your offers—The things you give away will also tell you what type of prospect you're getting. I'm willing to bet that the many different giveaways Dan Kennedy offers all bring him different types of prospects. A person signing up for a free e-mail series is a valuable prospect, certainly. But someone entering his National Sales Letter Contest to win that Mustang is someone who has digested his material, acted on it, and jumped through a major hoop by completing a lengthy application process. That person would be ten times more likely to spend serious money with Mr. Kennedy.

2.) **Get Them On Your List:** I learned this as a mantra from online marketing expert Alexandria Brown of www.queenscott.com. This is the way you learn who is reading your material and wants more of what you've got. Anything you offer in your book by way of a tool, report, audio, etc. should require the person to give you their contact information in order for them to get the offer. If you're doing this via the web, the email address is what you'll get. If you're sending a physical item, like a booklet or a free CD, then the person has to give you a full mailing address—which is perfect if you want to build a list for a direct mail campaign.

A Word About Shopping Cart/Database Management

You'll quickly learn, as your list grows, that your e-mail account may not allow you to send mass messages to groups larger than fifty to eighty. Also, it's not a good idea to only have your list on your computer. You'll want it backed up elsewhere. The solution: sign on for a list service. You'll have your database expertly maintained, plus most list services will give you templates and allow you to send out really good-looking HTML e-mail messages to your list. You can also get code and links that allow people to sign themselves onto your list from your Web site. There are many you can try. I use both Constant Contact (<u>www.constantcontact.com</u>) and 1 Shopping Cart (<u>www.scottshoppingcart.com</u>).

3.) **Allow You to Follow Up/Maintain Contact:** You'll want to keep in touch with the people on your list so they don't forget about you—and so you can offer them your products and services. The way you do it is up to you. A few ways to do this include...

Autoresponders—An autoresponder is a message/e-mail set up to go out automatically once a person signs up for your list. You can set up as many as you like for as long as you like in whatever intervals you like. A client of mine sends daily inspirational quotes. You could set up a free eight-week e-course related to your book subject as an autoresponder series. It's great because once you've done the work of creating and setting up the autoresponder, it can go out again and again without your doing anything more.

Newsletters or E-zines—I'm a big fan of e-mail newsletters because you can provide news on your activities and useful content for your readers. And you can send it out at little or no cost! When you provide content, such as tips for real estate investors, marketing ideas, or even cookbook recipes, you are further reinforcing your expertise. You're also giving people a good reason to stay on your list–they're getting good stuff out of it. You can also offer specials and market your upcoming events in your newsletter. In the past I have offered discounts on my services, gift certificates for people to give out over the holidays, and articles with career counseling and goal-achieving tips.

Direct Mailing—This is a pricier option, but often one that makes you memorable in the eyes of your prospect. You set up a series of mailings with three to four pieces in each mailing spaced ten to twelve days apart. If you make the letters and/or postcards in the campaign humorous and/or memorable through photos, stories, or an enclosed freebie, you can develop a rapport with your prospect that would have taken more time and effort to build in an online communication.

A Word about Your Web Site Strategy

If you're in the process of setting up a Web site for your book or your business that will capture names, I encourage you to take some extra time and do some strategic thinking here as well.

Usually when a Web site is built, you include an opt-in box where the person can sign up for whatever freebie you're offering. The person enters her contact information and receives a thank you e-mail and perhaps the information on how to get the material she just signed up for. The person gets the information and that's it. The process is over until she receives the next e-mail, newsletter, or autoresponder message from you.

I believe the time the person is in front of the computer signing up with you is a crucial time. Her interest is at its highest level. Obviously she is sitting there thinking about you and what you offer and she's already done some reading if she's decided to put her name and e-mail address in that little box. I say take advantage of this time as much as you can.

How? By thinking through a clear strategy for what happens after the person signs up. Yes, she can still get the thank yous and the information. But instead of sending her to a basic "thank you, your information is on the way" page, why not send her to a page that says "Thank you, it's great you're getting this important content. Are you ready for the next step? Then..." You can immediately **upsell** the prospect to the next level in your product funnel—a product setup where you have lower-priced, entry level products that lead to products and programs that successively increase in price for increasingly intensive experiences with you). That might be a $49 e-course, a $97 program with a workbook or a $297 home-study system.

Again, it can be tricky to figure all this out. Writing it down in a flow chart will help. The effort is worth it because you can get extra sales right off the bat just by asking for them! How great is that?

Design Your Lead Generation Strategy

Now it's time for you to start writing down the lead generation plan for your book. It may seem overwhelming, but stop for a moment and think about this: for all the time and effort you're putting into creating a book, you want that book to give you the biggest boost possible for your business. This is how you do it. The time figuring out your lead generation is well worth it! Remember to include the offers you'll make, the calls to action in your book, and how you'll follow up with your new prospects.

How much is a new customer worth to you? When you see the value in this, then you won't hesitate to make this next step. What extras could you offer in your book to entice new customers to contact you? Make sure you give them both online and offline options. Some people may be more open to faxing you their information rather than contacting you by e-mail. You'll also want the ability to reach them via regular mail as well as the Internet. The more marketing options you have available to you, the better.

CHAPTER 5

FISHING WHERE THE FISH ARE:
WHERE TO SELL YOUR BOOK

"Thrilled with having self-published my first book, I could feel the connections to be made with readers who would purchase my book and engage their faith in new ways. But getting it into their hands was going to be a challenge. Sophfronia encouraged me to call Christian and independent bookstores and ask if they would be interested in carrying my book. Quite wonderfully, this has turned out to be great advice. Eleven bookstores now share my book with their loyal customers! More so, with each contact at this personal level I am building enduring relationships and future possibilities for book signing and speaking engagements that will support my faith coaching practice as well as sales of my second book of essays due out later this year. Thanks, Sophfronia!"

Cory L. Kemp
Creating Women Ministries | Author, *You Don't See Many Chickens in Clearance:*
Essays on Faith and Living | www.creatingwomenministries.com

The editor-in-chief of *Publishers Weekly* said it, but I couldn't believe it. This was her keynote address to a meeting of the American Book Producers Association, and she was talking about "The State of Publishing Today." She pointed out that book sales were down, that everyone is trying different tactics, but

"Nobody really knows what works," she said.

She even described how there were too many instances of "me too-ism," in which publishers look at what books are selling and then come out with fifty similar titles. If they miss the moment and see that such books no longer sell, they may abandon projects or put no money into promoting them.

"Wait a minute," I thought. "What about the writer who has already written—and poured his heart and soul into—the book?" It sounds like he gets left holding the bag.

Then I was thinking about how writers, especially new ones, put so much faith in the opinion of publishers and agents. They believe the opinions of these professionals are validation, and they don't consider their writing successful or worthy unless a publisher says so.

But if no one in the industry really knows what works—or worse, if they're just following a current trend—how can you trust their evaluation of your manuscript? We've all heard stories of publishers being wrong before, of famous books that were rejected multiple times: Stephen King's *Carrie*, J.K. Rowling's first Harry Potter book, and E. Lynn Harris's *The Invisible Life*.

If you haven't heard it before, hear it now. **A rejection does not necessarily mean your book is unworthy!**

I don't fault anyone for not knowing what works. Publishing is a tricky business and selling to an ever-changing market is tough. What I question is how much influence we as writers give to others over how we feel about our own work.

Some entrepreneurs hesitate to self-publish their books because they hear the scary stories about "distribution"—which is how books get into the big bookstores such as Borders or Barnes & Noble. They know that it can be costly to hook up with a big distributor, which sends out sales reps and tells the stores why they should stock the book.

Okay, I know that sometimes being published by a traditional publisher may be a writer's goal because she wants the notice and status that comes of being promoted by a publishing house. But If the only thing keeping you from self-publishing your book is worrying about distribution, then know this:

The places where publishing houses are looking to increase sales are not in the big stores. They're in smaller, specialty markets where you wouldn't think to buy books: stores such as Office Depot, Office Max, Crate & Barrel, Anthropologie, or Urban Outfitters.

These stores are places not connected to the traditional distribution systems, **which means they are easier for self-published authors to approach on their own.** If you have a book with a specific target market (and as a businessperson, you should always know who your target market is), then it is often easier to find your market in specialty stores.

For instance, if you have written a leadership book, you might find more of your readers in gift shop of a hotel frequented by business travelers. If you were in a bigger bookstore, there would be more traffic, yes, but how many would be looking for a book such as yours?

One of my workshop students was very concerned about getting her book into big bookstores and had been calling buyers on her own with little success. Her book was religious in nature, so I suggested she call around to some of the giant churches that exist these days with humongous congregations. Many of them also have their own bookstores. Those stores have to be stocked just like any other bookstore. My student started calling them, and sure enough, she was able to sell her book to just about every one she contacted.

I want you to seriously consider alternative stores because this is considered the future of publishing. In the big leagues they're calling it "Continual Diversified Market Penetration." It just means they're going to put books wherever they can find the people who read them. So if a major publishing house were going to market your book this way, wouldn't it be better to do it yourself? And keep more of the money?

1. Get a pen and a sheet of paper right now and do a quick brainstorming list of specialty stores and catalogs where you think your reader would shop. The Sharper Image? Lillian Vernon? Bliss Spa? The Studio Museum of Harlem? Spencer Gifts? Office Max? Target?

2. I bet you've got yourself a pretty big list, right? Okay, now choose just one of the names, get on the phone, and find out who handles the buying for the store or catalog. Then make another phone call or send an e-mail to find out what you would have to do to get a book into that store or catalog.

Do this even if you haven't written or published your book yet! Why? Because once you understand what you have to do to get your book into stores, you'll be more inspired—and empowered—to complete your project. You'll know you'll be able to get your work to your readers and potential customers.

CHAPTER 6

BUZZ AND THE LUXURY OF FREE ADVERTISING

"Sophfronia has given me great insight into making my future book successful. I can't wait to have a chance to tap into the great depths of her knowledge."

H. Maggie Mayer, CPA
Mayer & Associates | www.maggiemayercpa.com | Madison, CT

Timothy Ferriss probably spent a good amount of money hiring assistants to research the top blogs on the Internet. He then dropped another chunk of change to go to conferences where he could meet some of these bloggers in person and chat them up about his upcoming book, *The 4-Hour Workweek*. But the buzz and publicity he unleashed when he got so many bloggers talking about his book? Priceless.

Mr. Ferriss also turned up on teleseminars hosted by some of the top names in the country including *Chicken Soup for the Soul* and *The Success Principles* author Jack Canfield. Then I saw him on television's *Regis and Kelly* with his tango partner breaking the world record for tango spins. He's been written up in the New York Times more than once. Mr. Ferriss got around, to say the least.

If you're planning a marketing campaign for your book then publicity will probably play an important role in that campaign. **Publicity is really free advertising**; other than getting a newspaper like the *New York Times* or a magazine such as *Fortune* or *Forbes* to do a story on you, the only other way to get into their pages is to buy advertising.

But publicity is a tricky thing and depends on many factors: timing of the news cycle, current trends, and current events. It's like trying to hop onto a moving train. Creating buzz as Mr. Ferriss did can give you a boost. There are a few other good ways to pursue publicity and we'll discuss those here.

Consider this chapter optional if publicity doesn't figure into your publishing plan. You might have different ideas for how you'll use your book. I have a client who didn't want to do much for his book beyond hosting a book signing party at his local library. He wasn't concerned about garnering tons of publicity because the purpose of his book was to be a big business card, something he could pull off the shelf to impress potential clients who came through his door. There's nothing wrong with that.

As a matter of fact, I would rather you had a solid publishing plan you stuck to instead of veering off course whenever anyone dangles a bright idea in front of you. That can happy often, especially once you get your freshly printed copy in your hands. You might feel like you want to run out and tell the world about it. Or not. But if you do, here's how you can go about doing it.

The Power of the Platform

Let's talk about platform first. As I said earlier, it's the magic word in publishing. When a publisher wants to buy, they're not just buying your book or your idea, they're buying you and the many ways you reach people. Some new authors focus solely on writing their books, thinking they can work on their platforms after the book is published. Unfortunately, the business doesn't work that way. You can't wait to sell your book to build a platform, because the platform is what helps sell your book. So get started now, even if you're still in the writing stage. Here's how you do it.

Decide On a Target Market

I'm going to keep reminding you of this important point because it's so tempting to skip this step, especially if you feel your book or story speaks to everyone. That may be, but it's awfully difficult–and expensive–to market to everyone. It doesn't mean you're shutting out potential customers, it just means you're focusing your laser to greatest effect. So if you survived two back surgeries and your story is about dealing with chronic pain, you may target people with back injuries, but that doesn't mean other sufferers of chronic pain (people with arthritis, for instance) will miss out on your message.

How Will You Talk to Your Market?

Thanks to the Internet you have many free and low-cost ways to communicate with your audience. Why is this important? Because this is how you establish yourself as an expert in your subject area. For instance, you may consider yourself an expert in back pain if you've developed ways to cope after having two surgeries. But you're a more visible expert with loads more credibility if you have a television show, newsletter, or radio program where you can discuss ways of dealing with chronic pain. And here's the best part–your show doesn't have to be on one of the big networks or even on cable. You can host your own show on the Web!

Likewise you can have your own radio show or podcast on the web. And blogs get tons of attention as well. This is important if you're not known in your field. Here's a great example: "Sportscaster Chronicles" is a blog and podcast by John Lewis, a New York City writer who is developing his platform as a sportscaster historian. You can view his handiwork at www.sportscasterchronicles.com/.

Send Out Press Releases

Don't keep it a secret. Let the media know you're an expert available to comment on relevant news stories. You don't want to send releases out without reason, though. For instance, almost all of John Lewis's sportscaster broadcasts are connected to something currently happening in the sports world. One time it was about comments that Bryant Gumbel made during the Olympics. Another was on the death of legendary sportscaster Curt Gowdy. Lewis can send press releases alerting reporters of the material especially when, as in Gowdy's case, he has unique information–John had interviewed Gowdy not long before his died.

Let's use the back pain story as another example. What if a popular painkiller is pulled from the market? You could send out a press release saying something like "10 Pain Relieving Exercises Developed for Former Users of Medicine X." Reporters love stuff like that. You've given them a fresh angle on a story they're already covering, without having to come up with any new material yourself. And when you write your query letter or book proposal, you get to include, "pain expert quoted in magazines and newspapers" among your list of qualifications. These days you can send a press release out via e-mail or use free distribution sites such as www.prfree.com, www.free-press-release. com, or www.i-newswire.com/submit.php.

Recently *USA Today* and ABC News did a weeklong series of stories on family members as caretakers of their elderly relatives. It hit home on many levels. It involved a huge chunk of the population: baby boomers. It involved commonality: more and more people are taking on the caretaker role. And of course it involved money: the costs both in time and dollars being expended, they reported, were a good chunk of change. I immediately contacted one of my workshop students who was working on a book about the care of Alzheimer's patients: it was the perfect time for her to send out press releases to get attention for her upcoming book. I know other authors with similar subject matter would do the same–if they were on top of their game.

This happens every time a big story hits the news. It's important you know this because the news always opens a brief window of opportunity for a writer to either pitch a book or get some television or radio time based on their expertise. But you have to be ready, even if your book isn't done. (You can always pitch yourself as "author of the forthcoming book..." Here's what you do.

1.) Keep Up On Current Events—TV and radio producers need new material and must put stories together quickly. That means you have to be right on top of the news and able to send a pitch in the moment you see a significant story developing. This doesn't mean you have to be glued to CNN daily or subscribe to an Associated Press news ticker, but you do have to be aware of what's going on. Speed is of the essence.

2.) Know How to Write a Quick Press Release—With that in mind, you'll have to be able to craft a good press release at a moment's notice. There are all sorts of technical aspects to putting together a press release, but basically you want it to have a strong headline, a quick and dirty description of your story and what you have to offer, and contact information so producers will know how to find you. Make sure you make the connection that you are a no-brainer to be interviewed. For instance, if you are a nurse who has worked with families struggling to care for loved ones with dementia, you could write a press release with the heading "Leading Expert Offers 4 Simple Strategies to Comfort a Confused Patient." Then you go on to outline a four-point plan. That's it. A producer can see an easy three-minute segment right there.

3.) Know How to Write a Quick Book Proposal—You'll want to be able to do the same with a book proposal. Here the most important part will be promoting your expertise and a great table of contents. The point is to catch an agent or editor's eye so they can start moving on the idea. You might have to flesh the proposal out after that, but for now you just want them to know you have the idea, expertise, connections, and ability to follow through with the book. (If you want help with this, go to www.doneforyouwriting.com/bookproposals.html to register for our next workshop on writing book proposals.)

4.) Use a Few Well-Chosen E-mail Addresses—Sure, you could mass e-mail a press release, but for your book proposal (and for certain media contacts) you'll want to make direct contact with a few, well-chosen people who you know will give your missive more than just a passing glance. This could be an agent you met in person at a conference, an editor who once rejected (with a nice note) one of your submissions, or a producer whose e-mail you received from a friend or colleague. Mark the e-mail "urgent" if you must because they understand when timing is important. Just don't do it every day! Ideally you want a person who can tell you pretty quickly if a project is viable, whether others want to do the same or if there's no interest period. Always be on the lookout to add such contacts to your list.

5.) Go!—You might have to do this again and again before hooking an agent, editor, or producer with your idea. Don't hesitate—and don't think, "Well, I didn't hear from this person before, so they won't be interested this time." You never know! Be confident in what you have to say–just make sure you *do* have something to say! There's no bigger turn-off for a producer or editor than to constantly receive disorganized, irrelevant information again and again from the same writer. Make sure yours is the pitch they pay attention to when it comes in.

Other Attention-Getters

Getting press isn't the only way you can get yourself in front of an audience. Keep these in mind as well.

Speak Your Mind

Speaking is a great way to get people familiar with you. If you fear speaking, think of it this way–pretend you are already on book tour and this is just another forum where you get to talk about your subject! You can start out speaking locally and doing it for free. If you're writing a memoir on your experiences in World War II, there may be high school history classes interested in hearing your story. Or, if you've learned how to cope with chronic pain, you could address support groups who deal with the same struggles. Speaking is also a great opportunity for adding people to your list so that you can let them know when your book comes out. Your list will always be an important marketing tool.

You don't have to have an elaborate PowerPoint presentation or music or flashing lights to be a speaker. Just choose one or two aspects of your story or subject (you don't want to give away your whole book!)

and start presenting them. Groups such as local Rotary clubs are always looking for speakers. If you feel you need to polish your skills, join a Toastmasters group. Bottom line, if you have a compelling story, some group large or small will want to hear it.

Publish Articles

You don't have to send a bunch of letters out to editors trying to get an assignment to write an article. You can write a meaty, content-filled article and distribute it on the Web. This is another way to establish your expertise. As with the press releases, there are many sites where you can make your articles (usually eight hundred to one thousand words in length) available for use in other Web sites, newsletters, and blogs. It's an excellent way to get your name in front of new audience members. Two popular distribution sites are www.ezinearticles.com and www.isnare.com.

If you find getting your articles formatted and submitted too time-consuming, you can always delegate the task. My assistant regularly submits my work with excellent results. I once had a reporter from *Investors Business Daily* call and interview me for a story after finding one of my articles that had been distributed through one of these sites.

Will You Pass the Test?

How does this all sound to you? If you're excited by these ideas and see them as opportunities to talk and write more about something you're deeply interested in, that's fantastic. It means you're on the right track— you've chosen a topic or story you're passionate about. If you aren't interested or motivated enough to want to speak and write articles or press releases connected to your topic, you may want to reconsider your book. After all, this is the kind of stuff you'll have to do at some point to sell your book. If you don't want to do it now, how will you sell your book later?

Even more to the point, if you're not willing or interested enough to put this kind of activity behind your book, why should a publisher be interested in working with you? You build your platform, you build your book's future. So give it your best shot. If you feel you need help brainstorming ideas or developing your plan, hire a coach or consultant to support you. Often it's easier to move forward when you can better see the road ahead.

Should You Hire a Publicist?

A publicist specializes in putting your work in front of the right audience and helping you establish relationships with the press and other media outlets. A well-connected publicist will have an easier job of getting someone important on the phone than you will.

Publicists have a bit of a bad name in the publishing world because some writers complain that they've spent all this money and aren't seeing any results. To avoid this trap, set clear outcomes and communicate them to your publicist. To set clear goals, you have to realize that the main task of your publicist is not so much to get your book into bookstores as to get you good press. He's going to help get your name out there.

Some factors to consider in gauging the success of your publicity campaign are:

1. the number of press clippings you gather
2. the new relationships you've developed
3. the appearances for which you've been booked

4. the growth of your mailing list.

By establishing clear goals, you have a clear measure of success. Tell your publicist the things you want up front, and avoid unnecessary resentments later.

A large publicity firm can charge anywhere from five thousand to seventy-five hundred dollars a month. Big-time celebrities can pay as much as ten thousand dollars a month. But, keeping in mind that what you're paying for are good contacts and staff, most authors can find good use in small, boutique firms that charge anywhere from one thousand to thirty-five hundred dollars a month. Sign a contract with your publicist in the beginning of your campaign, stipulating at that time how long the campaign will last. For instance, I worked with my first publicist for six months, and I paid her one thousand dollars a month for those six months.

I knew she was the right publicist for me because I had had an experience with someone who wasn't right for my book. A publicist once approached me from my e-mail list. She was interested in my book and wanted to work with me. I laid out for her a whole plan for what I wanted, an in-depth publicity campaign that was a little complicated because I was also promoting my life coaching work at the time and I wanted it all to be part of a single marketing effort. I printed up this list and showed it to her. Once she saw it, she was able to tell me she couldn't do it. And that was fine, no hard feelings, because if we hadn't communicated we'd both have been in some serious hot water.

I was able to go on and find another publicist and discuss this very same list with her, and she got it immediately. She came back with an outline for me on how we could bring this about, and we were able to start working together from page one. We both knew what we were doing. She knew what I expected from her and I knew what she expected of me.

The Press Kit

A press kit is the material that will help someone learn all about you and your book. Ideally, they'll learn all about your book without having to read anything, because we all know that there's already too much stuff for people to read. The press kit, therefore, is almost like a crib sheet to help a reporter interview you or generate publicity around the book without her having to do too much work on her own.

A lot of first-time authors assume that their publicist will put the press kit together. But the fact is that you have to provide most of the materials necessary to your publicist or publisher in order for them to build your press kit. If you're being published by a traditional publisher, your publicist may ask you to fill out an author questionnaire to help him design your campaign. I'll include some of the questions here so you can see some of what's considered important to know:

- Educational background

- Honors, citations, or prizes

- Names and/or occupations of family members, if newsworthy or relevant

- Avocations, hobbies, or special interests, anything relevant to your book

- Foreign countries in which you have resided or traveled

- Cities and states in which you've lived

- Inspiration for your book

- Favorite authors

- Any classic or popular books that seem to have the same kind of readership you want to attract

- Current books or works in progress that you know of which might compete with your book for public attention

- Feathers that distinguish your book from others on the subject

A press kit begins with a press release, explaining the highlights of your book and even touching on why you're the best person to be writing this book. Your press kit should also include:

- a great author bio, one that both demonstrates your expertise and reflects what an interesting person you are, so that you can land an interview.

- a "canned Q & A," which will help an interviewer do an interview quickly without much preparation. To create your Q & A, you get to determine what questions you'd like to answer in an interview.

The canned Q & A is actually a very prevalent interview tactic in both the print and television media. In television talk shows, the producer or production assistant will have called the guest beforehand to ask questions and to get these stories out of them. That's why Dr. Phil likes to tell his guests, "You know I'm not going to ask questions that I don't already know the answer to."

In addition, your press kit should contain

- a list of endorsements and testimonials. These will include your celebrity and author blurbs and reviews from colleagues who read your book and really liked it.

- A 5x7 photograph in which you look like a really engaging, open-eyed person ready to take on the world is also necessary. I encourage all of my clients to have photos taken professionally and I suggest you do the same. A great photo sells more books than you realize. Plus you can use the picture again and again on other products and promotional materials such as your Web site. This is definitely money well spent.

Finally, your press kit will include any marketing or promotional items that make your package stand out among the rest. Maybe it will be a snazzy bookmark or a little bracelet, something that will make the recipient open the package and say, "Oh this is interesting. What's this about?"

You can also put your press kit online. I have an online press kit, and I think it's important for authors to make one. Your online press kit contains all of the same stuff in the paper press kit, but you make it available on your Web site. You can save postage costs by pointing people to the site. There you have Web- or print-ready pictures, text, etc.

If you check out Timothy Ferriss's online press kit at http://fourhourworkweek.com/ferriss-pressroom.htm, you'll see he's made available the front and back images of his book jacket as well as a variety of print-ready pictures of himself. This gives the publication a variety to choose from. When my first novel, *All I Need to Get By*, came out I learned that some magazines, like *People*, don't want to use the photo on the book jacket. So when you get those professional photos taken, don't choose just one.

If a media outlet wants to have a traditional press kit, they will let you know. Perhaps they need the actual kit to take into a meeting to pitch an editor directly on you and your book. You'll never know what anyone will want. Just be prepared.

Your Big Debut: Media Appearances

If all goes well, the outcome of working with a publicist and creating a stunning press kit is that you will appear in the media. You're going to be on radio and television talking about your book. If you're a speaker and used to the spotlight, great! If you're not used to the spotlight and, even worse, have just spent months cocooned in your office typing away at your book, you might show up for your first interview looking like a deer caught in a car's headlights. That's pretty bad because if you have a horrible interview those producers won't ask you back. The idea is for you to be totally prepared so you can focus on smiling and being an interesting and engaging interview.

To prepare for media engagements, you must create specific **talking points** for yourself, things you know you must say on air no matter what happens. Your talking points should include:

- the title of the book

- your Web site information

- a compact sound bite that communicates your book's central message.

This is important because reporters won't always ask the right questions. And you might be nervous in front of the microphone or on camera. An interview can be over in five minutes and then you realize, "Oh, I didn't mention my Web site," or "Gosh, we didn't even repeat the title of the book." It's important to write those things down and have them in front of you all the time, or just repeat them to yourself over and over so that you know to say them when you're on air.

I believe that you should accept interviews even if they're small and in far away places because

1. you never know who could be listening and
2. it will give you great practice for when the big interview shows start requesting your presence.

Recently I was interviewed for a feature in my local paper, the Newtown *Bee*. It's a little paper and only appears weekly. But just two days later I walked into a coffee shop and a woman saw me and said, "Weren't you in the *Bee*?" I said that I was and she replied, "My husband runs a speakers bureau and I saw your article. I think you'd be a great speaker for his bureau." I said, "Well, I do speaking engagements," handed her my card, and told her to have her husband call me. Now that wouldn't have come about if I hadn't been in the *Bee*. That's just to illustrate that you never know who's going to be reading, listening, or watching.

If you find that you do have a lot of media stuff on your calendar, I recommend getting some media training. I think it's important, but it can be expensive as well. If you can't hire a media trainer, get a friend or a family member to videotape you. You can just sit in a chair talking and pretend that you're being interviewed. Afterwards you can study the tape.

You're going to be looking for any facial ticks or extraneous movement that you didn't realize you were making. Perhaps your hands were moving up and down all the time and you didn't even realize it because you were just so excited while you were talking. You also want to practice having a straight and steady gaze at your interviewer. When I watched my first television interviews, I noticed my big brown eyes looked like little marbles bouncing all over the place. So I learned to be more focused in the way I trained my gaze.

It's also important to learn how to dress for TV. A media trainer can give you some tips. For women, even if you don't wear a lot of makeup, you still need to learn how to put it on. Learning how to put on camera-ready makeup is important, because when you do TV you won't always have a makeup artist there to do it for you. One of the best investments I ever made was taking a modeling class when I first got out of college. I learned how to put on makeup, how to walk, and how to dress. I also learned how to punch up my makeup to be on camera, a skill that has come back to work for me countless times when I had to look good and do it on my own.

One More Thing

Have fun! I must remind you to do that during this process. This is, after all, what you've been working on so hard for so long. Every interview is an opportunity. Every minute in front of a camera is your chance to glow and share your message—and your business—with the world.

PART III

HOW TO CRAFT A CROWD-PLEASING BOOK

I've dissected many successful books, all of which have commonalities that you can put to use to make your book just as effective and reader-friendly. To help you do this I created the **Book Building Circle**. The circle will help you organize your material. It's different from other methods in that it's not just a basic chapter-by-chapter outline. In fact, you can think of it as organization without the outlining!

This method allows you to look at your book as a whole and then break it up into its purpose and its functioning pieces. You build the book

- section by section and

- with the overall goal of the book in mind.

It's a powerful exercise and makes for a powerful book. If you look carefully at the bestsellers of our times, you'll see that in one way or another they can be broken up and their parts placed within the sections of this circle and pyramid. The books work as a whole because the smaller parts have been well considered and superbly crafted. You'll find that if you work through your book with this circle in mind, the book will practically write itself!

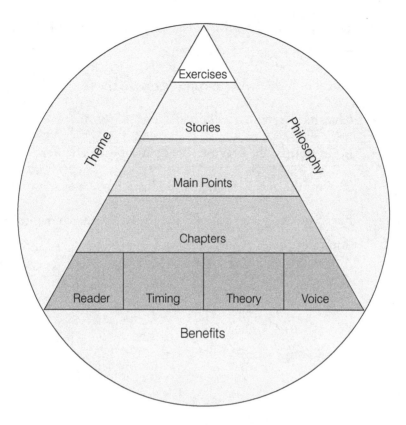

Here's a brief preview of all the sections of the circle and the pyramid enclosed. We'll start with the circle since that's also where you'll begin.

- **Benefits**: what the reader will get from the book

- **Philosophy**: your view of the world

- **Theme**: the subject you're talking about, expressing your philosophy all the while

- **Reader:** who the reader is

- **Timing:** the time frame you are discussing

- **Theory:** your idea of how your philosophy should be implemented in regards to the Theme

- **Voice:** how you wish to come across to the reader

- **Chapters:** how you will divide your subject matter

- **Main Points:** the organized content of each chapter

- **Stories:** the anecdotes that will illustrate your main points

- **Exercises:** how you will get the reader to put your information to use

CHAPTER 7

WHY READ YOUR BOOK?
PHILOSOPHY, THEME, AND BENEFITS

"Sophfronia has a winning combination of real experience, incisive clarity, strategic and doable suggestions, encouragement, and human warmth."

Annicka Henttonen Steiner

www.integrativehealing.ch | Basel, Switzerland

Benefits

We start here, at the bottom, the foundation of everything, because this is where new authors often make their first and biggest mistake: they think they know best what the book should be about. And it's easy to see how this mistake can be made. Your name is on the book. Your face is on the book. The book is all about your information, your stories, and your expertise. But—and you may need to sit down for this one—**your book is not about you!**

When a reader first picks up your book, most likely he has never heard of you. He didn't pick up the book because he recognized your name or your face. He picked it up because the title indicated that the book is going to help him with something he really, really wants help with. You're offering a solution. Your mission as an author is to offer him something of value which, in one way or another, will change his life for the better. It will alter him. It will improve him. It will inform him. You've made it obvious that the reader will come away from the book with specific steps, a definite plan—an answer!

Just look at one of Dr. Phil McGraw's books. On the cover of *Family First* it is crystal clear what the reader will get because it's stated in the subtitle: "Your Step-by-Step Plan for Creating a Phenomenal Family."

A reader will pick up that book and say, "I want a phenomenal family. I'm going to read this because Dr. Phil is going to tell me exactly how to do it. He's going to take me by the hand, step by step. It seems like it's going to be easy and rewarding, so I'm going to buy this book."

The subtitle extends a real core benefit to the reader. The benefit is clear, presented in a how-to, step-by-step process. In my experience, the best nonfiction books are the ones that deliver really well on the promise of a system. People want to be taken by the hand and shown how to do something. We are all bombarded daily with information on what we must do: lose weight, attain our goals, make more money, get a better job, spend more time with our families, invest in real estate, whatever. But it's never obvious how to do these things. The reason? Smart business owners and entrepreneurs **sell the how**. They know this is the part that people will pay for!

To this end, it's also important for you to be tuned in to your audience enough to know what "how" they are most interested in and **willing to pay** to get. This knowledge may come to you just from working your business. You might notice that people are coming to you to solve the same problem over and over. One of my clients is a marketing expert, but she started out as a nutrition and wellness expert. She had a difficult time getting clients until she committed herself to learning how to market herself. As she became more and more successful, others in her field came to her to find out what she was doing and how they could use her methods to get more clients as well.

She eventually hit critical mass where the bulk of her work came from coaching around developing a business and marketing and not from the nutrition and wellness. Her market had spoken to her and told her what they needed and were willing to pay for. She eventually wrote a book, again based on all the knowledge and expertise she acquired from coaching so many and learning firsthand what their challenges were.

If you are still relatively new to your business and getting to know your market, it may help to just survey your customers. (My client, mentioned above, does this all the time to great success!) Just ask them what they're biggest challenges are, what they want to learn, what they feel they need the most help with. There are many online tools to help you do this and analyze the results quickly and easily. One is www.SurveyMonkey.com.

Your book demonstrates your expertise with "the how." The reader learns to trust you and your process because you're laying it all out for her. This makes it easier for her to make future decisions to buy more from you or to work with you personally.

Think in Steps, Keys, and Strategies

Composing your book in steps makes your job easier as well because you know exactly what you're doing. You won't lose track of what you have to say, and you won't get overwhelmed by a bunch of research. You will be forced to keep returning to the fact that you've outlined five, or six, or nine steps; and no matter what else you're doing or think you're doing with this book, you have to walk your reader through these steps—and they have to work!

You might be thinking, "Yeah, but what I have to write about doesn't work that way." That's okay. Even if you're not presenting it to the reader as a step-by-step process, I challenge you to think of your work in this way to help you to organize the chapter-by-chapter flow of your book. Even stories are told a particular way—beginning, middle, and end—in order to give readers a very particular experience—to give the reader high notes and low notes and draw them into the story.

You can think of your material in this way. Fabienne Fredrickson of www.ClientAttraction.com teaches this as figuring out your "proprietary system." Your "system" is simply what you do when you work with clients all the time.

How to Create Your Process and/or Program

If you do have information but haven't organized it into your process or program yet, here are a few pointers on how to do it.

1. Identify your "Point A" and "Point B." Ideally you are writing your book to help the reader get from one place to another; to go from one way of thinking to another; to go from one action to another. What is that point? What is the goal?

2. Have you made this journey yourself? This is the case for many speakers, entrepreneurs, and small business owners. You did it yourself; people are coming to you because you succeeded and they want to do it exactly the way that you did. So do a detailed examination of how you traveled the journey. Identify all the key stops, decisions, or actions you made along the way.

3. Now organize your key stops, decisions, or actions into the steps that others can take. If you have problems doing this and you work with clients all the time, just think about how

you work with your clients. Are there particular steps you do with every single one? My guess is there are, but you've never thought about it as a process because it's what you always do. But there's another word to call what you always do: a system. And people pay big bucks for systems!

Once you've completed this process, take a good look at the system you've created because you're going to use it all the time from now on! These steps will be the steps you use to organize your speeches, to create products, to create workshops. Every offering will be some form of your process. One offering may be longer or one may be shorter. You can teach a weeklong workshop or do a ninety-minute talk. You can expand and contract your material as needed.

Philosophy

Philosophy is your idea of how the world should work. Ideally, philosophy is a far larger realm than theme. Your philosophy of life is how you believe people should live; for example, maybe how people should eat, or maybe how people should treat the environment.

As an example, we're going to use Dr. Phil McGraw's book, *Family First*. Dr. Phil's philosophy is, "Be in charge of your life," and that one philosophy is pretty much the same in all of his books including *Relationship Rescue*, *Life Strategies*, and *The Ultimate Weight Loss Solution*. Notice how each of these books addresses different themes like relationships, life coping, and weight loss. Theme, therefore, is different than philosophy. Theme is how you will organize the expression of your philosophy.

Dr. Phil has one philosophy, but in each book he chooses a different theme through which to express it. In *Family First* that just happens to be the theme of family being the sacred foundation on which to build an amazing life and an amazing society.

His philosophy, "Be in charge of your life," means that you have a choice in everything that you do. He expresses that philosophy in *Life Strategies*, for instance, by promoting learning to take responsibility for our lives and who we are. *Relationship Rescue* is all about taking responsibility for your place in your relationships, and partners learning more about each other. In *Family First*, that philosophy is discussed through the theme of being in charge of your family, taking responsibility for having a great family, and being a leader.

If you're having trouble with this concept, think of it this way: philosophy is like the ground you stand on, while the theme is the direction you walk in. On the same ground, you could walk north, south, east, or west to explore different avenues of the same ground.

Your philosophy comes down to the questions we return to again and again throughout this book: *What do you have to say to the world? What message do you want to put out there?* You can only come up with that by thinking about who you are. This requires activities like meditating, journaling, or just paying attention to what you're already extending out into the world. If you have preferences for certain movies or certain radio shows, all of those preferences originate in the fact that you see the world in your own unique way.

Tuning into that uniqueness will help you decide what your book will be about. Your uniqueness is what allows you to say, "I really do have something to offer the world." That's what inspires you to put a book together in the first place. You have a burning passion to get that message out no matter what it takes.

What's great about philosophy is that it doesn't have to be just about you. That passion spurs you to action because your message can help other people; it will really turn into something special when it is read and grasped by thousands or even millions.

However when you think about philosophy, you'll find it isn't necessarily front and center. It's not something you're going to put in a book proposal, for example. This isn't something Dr. Phil walks around directly promoting. His philosophy is coming from within; this is the thing that could be *motivating* you quietly but consistently, like a coach on the sidelines. It's not something you go shouting around town. People don't take it very well when other people are hitting them over the head with their personal philosophies.

Theme

That's where theme comes in. If, in your nonfiction book, you're couching your philosophy in the terms of helping to solve a problem, offering solutions or explanations of the way things are, that's more acceptable to readers than watching someone shaking a finger at them saying, "You should do this. You should live like this."

People relate to theme because it brings philosophy right home to where their concerns are. Dr. Phil really does exude this essence of personal responsibility, but how does that relate to me? As a reader of his books, I would consider how I want to improve my relationships. So I read his book and I get that the core of it is taking personal responsibility. And this leads us back to the beginning of the Book Building Circle that surrounds the pyramid, which are the benefits, what the reader gets out of the book. See how this all works, how it all ties together?

CHAPTER 8

SPEAKING TO THE READER
THE READER, TIMING, THEORY, AND VOICE

"Sophfronia is on the cutting-edge of getting your revelation to become your manifestation. The information she provides is priceless and she certainly has a passion to see others get published. I would never have become a published author without her coaching and inspiration."

Dr. M. James Masterson Sr.
Author, *Factors of Our Faith* | Stafford, VA

The Reader

The pyramid in the Book Building Circle begins with a wide foundation comprised of four separate cornerstones. The first cornerstone at the pyramid's base is your reader. A book, especially a nonfiction book, is a way to forge a relationship. In fiction, you have all sorts of characters running around and doing things, but in a nonfiction book, the main characters are usually just the writer and the reader. You have to think about what type of relationship you want to develop with your reader.

Is this a teacher/student relationship? A peer-to-peer relationship? Is it a storytelling relationship? If you're doing a biography, for instance, is the relationship that of a storyteller to listener? You must always be asking yourself, "To whom am I speaking? How do I want to speak?"

Consider what it's like to walk down a path side by side in intimate conversation with a friend versus sitting in a classroom or a lecture hall listening to an amazing speaker. Those are just a few of the different ways you can imagine this relationship, or your position vis a vis the reader.

Timing

The next cornerstone to consider is timing. By this I mean your choice of placing your book in the past, present, or future. For instance, if you're writing a biography, then typically everything in the book is about the past. You're telling a story of something that's already happened. Or your book could be set in the present if you're telling a story about a current crisis, such as the Hurricane Katrina disaster. Finally, a book could be set in the future if you're putting forth an idea about future economic trends.

This book moves between the present (what I'm suggesting you now) and the future (what you will do with your book). In *Family First*, Dr. Phil makes use of all three—past, present, and future. He discusses his past experiences with his own family; he talks about the way families are living now, examining issues like over-scheduling, not having dinners together, and lack of communication; finally, he talks about the future in terms of where these patterns could lead if you don't get your family back together.

Understanding this timing concept is important because one of the most common mistakes new writers make is getting verb tenses wrong. They use past tense verbiage when they should use present, or they flip inexplicably between tenses. If you make your timing choices up front it will make you more aware of your tenses as you're writing.

You'll be able to correct mistakes quickly or, even better, not make them at all.

Theory

Our third cornerstone at the pyramid's base of the Book Building Circle is theory. Theory is how the writer is proposing to make the theme play out in the reader's life.

For example, we know the theme of *Family First* is family. It's about children being protected and making your home a safe place. But how do we make that happen? Dr. Phil's theory about how to make that happen is "Every family needs a hero. That one person has to step up to the plate and say, "This isn't working and something has to change." Somebody has to be the leader. From the theme of family, therefore, follows his *theory* that family issues are most fruitfully and sustainably managed by someone in the family who takes a leadership role. Of course, this ties back into his philosophy of taking control of and responsibility for one's own life.

In Anthony Robbins's book *Awaken the Giant Within,* his theme is, like Dr. Phil's, that you are in control of your decisions and that you can really tap into your human potential. Well, how do you do that? Robbins's is that you must become aware that you are in control of everything that happens within you. You are in control of your emotions, of making choices, of how you're going to feel about a certain thing. You're in control of creating what he calls "neuro associations" that will draw you towards a positive behavior or help you move away from a negative behavior. That's his *theory*. He draws in a scientific aspect to his *theme*, which everyone else sees as being based on heart and art, by explaining how the human brain works.

I'm assuming if you've already decided to write a nonfiction book that you have a plan you're presenting to the world. But let's say you're still far away from doing your book proposal or writing your book. You haven't worked out your theories. Ideally, your theme and your theory are things that you've learned by living life. Nonfiction books are often the result of what you do in your everyday life; for example, you may notice that things could work better if people did things in a different way.

I have a client who is a mortgage broker and very involved in real estate investing. In developing the content for his book we saw that he would have a *theme* about people's becoming educated about the process of investing in real estate, and why it's good, etc. His *theory* of why people have trouble with this is that they don't understand credit; they don't understand the way credit works, and they don't understand their own credit. So in order for him to make all the great real estate investing stuff happen, his book teaches people in detail the ins and outs of credit. He's arrived at his theory from his personal experience talking to clients about their finances and just being struck by how little people know and understand their credit.

Notice that it is not enough just to say, "People don't know enough about how to buy a house." Anybody can say that. But what are you going to teach me about it? What's unique about your perspective? Your theory is your own **unique selling proposition**, or your angle that is unique in the market.

Maybe your how-to just makes more sense, or it fits readers better than somebody else's theory. I'm always interested in how so many books—Stephen Covey's, Anthony Robbins's, Wayne Dyer's—all say the same things on a certain level, but they speak to it in different ways. Maybe you don't hear it when you read Stephen Covey, but you totally hear the message from Anthony Robbins, or vice versa. Or Stephen

Covey just totally hit home for you but maybe you would not have read that message if you had gotten it from Caroline Myss's *Anatomy of the Spirit*.

One author can even explore the same subject over the course of many books. Zig Ziglar explored "the top" from many different angles, starting with *See You at the Top* and following it with *Over the Top* and *What I Learned on the Way to the Top*. The differences in these books show how Mr. Ziglar's views on "the top" changed over time. He responded to the idea, which I'm sure he experienced himself, of *what happens now I'm at the top?* He couldn't have written *Over the Top* without exploring how to get to the top.

Music is the same. Take a pianist like Arthur Rubenstein. If you heard a recording of his playing and then went to hear him live, you would hear a completely different interpretation of the same piece. It's not the same as the recording he did twenty years ago because he always plays each piece differently, every single time. In the same sense, an author can really explore a topic from different angles. That's why so many authors, when they get going, can write ten to fifteen books, or more, over the course of a lifetime.

This happens because the musician and the writer are **living and growing new themes** so they will have new educational experiences and new thought processes to bring to their writing and their music. Each pass will be different, bringing a greater heft of maturity, perhaps making something deeper and more interesting, or even 180 degrees going the other direction. It's fascinating to watch that journey of creativity and discovery.

That's why it's important for a writer to have his own ideas and not borrow them from someone else. It truly is about what *you're* bringing to the book, how much you're putting yourself into it, because that's what brings energy and vitality to your work. That's what creates relationships between readers and writers, and that's what makes a lasting impression on the world.

Voice

With this cornerstone, we're talking about the writer's voice. How do you want to use your voice in your book? With someone like Dr. Phil or myself, the voice is going to sound just like we're talking to you in person. Dr. Phil has a very specific voice, and I bet writing a book for him is probably almost like writing a letter except that he's giving out some heavier, more organized information. When we buy a book like *Family First*, it's the personality that we're buying. We're buying Dr. Phil's voice.

If you're writing a biography, for example, you have to ask yourself whether you want your voice to be as evident. Maybe you're writing so that your personality is in the background, but you still want a strong style of writing and some strong storytelling skills with which to weave the tale of a person's life.

There are different levels of formality with voice. A biography can have a formal setup but also an engaging, storytelling feel. There are so many types of nonfiction, and your voice will vary depending on the type you're writing. Truman Capote employed his strong storytelling voice when he wrote *In Cold Blood*. That was nonfiction, but he was telling a story. It wasn't written in a casual voice; he used the feel of a novel to tell a very real story.

You can also swing in the other direction and employ an academic voice, which is traditionally supposed to be totally devoid of human personality. Academic-speak is a language in and of itself. In deciding which type of voice you're going to "put on" for your work, you have to understand the type of effect that you want to have, and to whom you're speaking.

Sometimes you can play around with what you're doing, so voice always requires your consideration. Edmund Morris, who wrote an autobiography of Ronald Reagan (*Dutch*), actually placed himself within the narrative as a character. It was quite controversial at the time. But when you're working for a certain effect, sometimes you have to go out on the edge. You don't make an arbitrary choice, by any means, but you do make the choice that is the best for the book.

CHAPTER 9

DIVIDING IT ALL UP: YOUR CHAPTERS, MAIN POINTS AND STORIES

"Sophfronia taught me everything I needed to know to go forward writing and publishing my book. She is encouraging and positive but constructively critical when needed."

Beverly Moore, RN, CS
Quincy, MA | Author of *Matters of the Mind...and the Heart:*
Meeting the Challenges of Alzheimer Care | www.AlzheimerCoachingServices.com

Chapters

The next level on our Book Building Pyramid is all about building chapters. Chapters are your main tool for organizing your book. This is pretty easy to do with nonfiction since most real-world topics can be broken up into steps, strategies, periods, and so on. You can even go beyond chapters and have your book segmented into parts. For instance, *Family First* has part one and part two, and there are chapters within those two parts. This book has three parts.

I'm often asked how many chapters a book should have. There is no hard and fast rule. It all depends on your material and how you want to present it to the reader. When you begin outlining a possible table of contents for a book, I suggest to my clients that they start with ten or twelve chapters. Once they start dividing up their subject matter they can tell what works best. If they don't have enough material to fill ten chapters, then fewer will do. If they find the ten chapters are packed and each chapter is thirty pages, then maybe using more chapters to break up the book more would be ideal. However long your chapters, you'll want to make sure that each chapter has a specific purpose. This chapter, for example, has the purpose of showing you how to divide up your book.

It might help you to write out each of your chapter titles and then make a list under each one of what the chapter needs to cover. This will be your list of **main points**, the next level of the pyramid. Once you write the chapter you can go over this list again to see if the chapter has succeeds in doing what you want it to do.

Main Points

The meat of the chapters happens in this next layer of the pyramid. Main points, besides voice, are what the reader is coming for. These are where you detail the step-by-step things that your readers must do in order to reach the result that they want. For instance, *Family First* provides some steps to make your family better. Dr. Phil tells you about developing a sense of security in your home, about putting your family on project status, and how to help your kids set goals. He goes step by step and tells you how to do each of those things.

Let's look more closely at how this book is organized. Within chapter one, "Family Matters," he's describing *why* this subject matter is so important. How do you get into the mindset of wanting to put your family first? Then, in chapter two, he gives some specific strategies for divorced and blended families, which have very specific challenges. In chapter three, he lists and explains five factors for a phenomenal family, and that's where he talks about security and putting your family on project status. He also has a chapter about parenting style and how to evaluate the type of parent that you are.

The point is that each chapter of your book ideally will give readers some really meaty points of focus and methods to help them realize your concepts in real life. Once that is done you can move on to the next chapter. Each chapter should build on the last one, and all of your chapters will work together to paint a broader picture—namely, the philosophy we talked about earlier.

Stories: Why Anecdotes Are Important

Building on our main points layer, we're now going to add a crucial ingredient, stories. How do you bring those main points alive for the reader? How do you make them real? By telling stories.

An **anecdote** is defined as a short and amusing or interesting story about a real person. They're really all around us: we tell them at cocktail parties, around the water cooler at work, at the bar with our friends. Nonfiction books, especially how-to books, are chock full of them. But because they're all around us, I think we tend to take anecdotes for granted. We also don't think about what they can really do.

A story is probably one of the strongest teaching tools there is. This idea goes all the way back to the Bible and beyond: we learn best from stories. It helps to hear how someone else handled the same situation we're currently dealing with because we can see what is possible. It's also the best way to understand complex concepts because you get to "see" them in action.

Here's an example to illustrate the power of the anecdote. Author Michael Gerber first published the hugely successful book, *The E-Myth: Why Most Small Businesses Don't Work and What To Do About It* in the 1980s. It was updated and published as *The E-Myth Revisited* in 1995.

This was the book I read first, and I was curious to see the original version. I wondered, "How has the world of small business changed since the 1980s and what does Michael Gerber have to say about it?"

With the help of my local library I hunted down an old copy of *The E-Myth*. As I thumbed through it, I was shocked to see that Gerber's opinions, advice, and strategies were almost exactly the same. But there was one, quite significant addition to *The E-Myth Revisited*, and with her came many, many eye-opening moments: her name is Sarah.

Throughout the new edition of his book, Michael Gerber illustrates his concepts by telling the story of a pie baker named Sarah. She loves baking pies so much and does it so well that she opens a pie shop. The tale unfolds from there in every chapter of the book. You even get to sit in on the coaching sessions she has with the narrator and watch her implement what she learns. Her example is so powerful that today small business owners can discuss their companies with each other and use phrases such as "but I'm still baking all the pies myself," and they perfectly understand each other.

Sarah and her long-running anecdote brought the E-Myth to life and made millions more entrepreneurs see how they could apply its methods in their businesses. Her story is emotional, informative and inspiring. You want your anecdotes to work the same way.

Choosing the Right Anecdotes

As you outline your book, make a note as to what story or stories you will tell to illustrate every point you'll be making. Tell the stories of your clients (changing names, of course, to protect their privacy) or use anecdotes from your own life experience.

This is really where you get to showcase your expertise and let people see that you know how to solve their problem because you've done it before and for people in exactly their situation. Make sure you use the right stories. You want them to be clearly connected to your concept so there's no mistaking your point.

A good anecdote has:

- a clear protagonist (meaning the story is about one person)

- a strong "before" description (as in, "Here's what was going on with this person before you or your strategy showed up.")

- a clear and simple description of what specific action plan the person used to change the situation

- a powerful "after" description of how the person's life was different, better, more prosperous, etc. Ideally you want this to be inspiring, so that the reader wants very much to have that "after" description for themselves.

Stories and anecdotes highlight, or bring home, the points that you're making in each chapter. Dr. Phil does this by using his own personal stories about growing up. Some of the stories are pretty touching. He grew up in a family that had very little money, many challenges, and an alcoholic father. He had a lot of problems connecting with his family, but these very stories help you to see that he knows what he's talking about from *experience*, and that these are issues that he's dealt with himself. So the reader is more connected to the book and the information because the stories Dr. Phil reveals about his own family.

What we're touching on here is something that's called **social proof**. What that means is that when you hear other people who have had similar experiences, or they've had the same problem and they got great results based on a certain method of resolution, it adds that much more credibility to the maxim "If they did it, I can do it, too." Social proof is powerful because often times it is the one thing that makes people act.

The message here is this: don't be afraid to use stories in your nonfiction. Use them early and use them often, because they're what engage the reader most fully. Think of it as a rhythm you're drumming out between points and illustrations, ideas and anecdotes. Now, every story in your nonfiction book won't make people cry, and you don't want them to. The story simply has to make a point; it doesn't have to be long or huge to be powerful. Everything is a mix; it's coming up with a good mix that's the challenge.

CHAPTER 10

EXERCISES: HOW TO GET YOUR READER MOVING

"Sophfronia's tips have inspired me to get cracking on my nonfiction book as I can see how it will almost certainly boost my business."

Cherry-Ann Carew
Huntington Beach, CA

Now we've arrived at the Book Building Pyramid's pinnacle, the compact point that arises from the foundation. This is the most focused part of the book because this is where you get the reader to use your material. You might ask the reader to take steps by writing in the book. You might ask the reader to change a behavior or to experiment with a new tool. Basically this is where the writer is telling the reader, "Here's what you do with this information, here's how you make it work." What's great about this is that readers will begin to see your value and expertise if they start using your suggestions and having some success with them.

Exercises are very specific. For instance, in *Family First*, in one of the chapters about the five factors of a phenomenal family, Dr. Phil tells you what to do when a crisis strikes. In other words, here's how you use all of his information when something horrible happens in your family. First, he says, "Be prepared." He tells you how to look for warning signs; he tells you to stay calm and to remain in charge of yourself, and how this will inspire confidence and reassurance in the rest of your family. He tells you to remove danger, which might be done by calling the police or confiscating dangerous things, or preventing your child from having contact with certain people. Then he says, "Work the problem, not the person." He tells you to communicate, and in a step-by-step procedure, he explains exactly how you take care of it.

Exercises should occur throughout your book because you're not just telling people to do one thing in one situation. That's not really how nonfiction books work. You're dealing with one problem but many different issues will surround any given problem, because that is the way life is. Things that may attack your family, for example, will come from more than one direction; therefore, you're going to want to put many different action plans throughout your book.

Let's take as an example a weight loss book. Say your theory is about how to avoid overeating. Well, throughout the book you're going to give readers different strategies about how to avoid overeating in restaurants, how to avoid overeating at bedtime, how to avoid overeating at buffets, or whatever. Those action plans will be happening throughout the book.

In some nonfiction books the author will present questions and free space to make notes in at the end of every chapter. It makes readers stop and absorb what they just learned and even to design their own plans based on their unique circumstances. I find more and more books don't just ask questions; they're coming right out and saying, "Stop right now and do this." How many ways can you do the same in your book?

CHAPTER 11

GETTING THE FIRST DRAFT DONE

"I appreciate Sophfronia's willingness to share so many golden nuggets! I was blown away by her fantastic strategies. She reinforced how critical it is to invest time in strategies for lead generation and building an audience before becoming published. I can really see how this is an area in which there can be huge payoffs and certainly worth the effort."

Lily De Rehe
www.lusciouslife.com.au | New South Wales, Australia

There are three benefits to finishing your first draft that I'd like to alert you to before you take the plunge and start writing it.

First: **rewriting is easier than writing**. Obviously, in a revision, you have something there to work with. There's no blank screen to contend with; just having something on paper, even if it's all the wrong stuff, will spur you to action because you're immediately asking yourself, "How can I make this better?"

Second: when your first draft is done, suddenly your book is real. You now have something to offer, even if you wouldn't show it to anyone yet. It's now something you can look to with confidence. If you meet an editor or an agent, for instance, you can say to him, "I'm working on a book and I have something. It's in the rough stages but I can polish it up and send you the first three chapters if you're interested."

Finally, you have something to show. It's no longer an abstract idea. It's real, and you have it on paper.

Third: through the course of writing your draft, you have learned not to be afraid of words. The reason for this is that you're going to be doing this draft very quickly. In the process your command over words naturally increases, you learn more about the words, and you learn more about writing. In fact, you may not realize it now, but you learn about the whole process: you're learning how to work. This helps stave off writer's block because you're just throwing words on the page just to see what will stick. Sometimes I will start off by writing nonsense. It's my story, but it's almost like I'm talking to myself or writing notes. The point is just to get something down so I can work with it.

The speed with which you finish your first draft will depend on you. Some people can pound out a draft in a month, and for others that's just not possible. If you can just do a few pages a day, you can have a first draft in six months. Regardless, the idea is to move along as fast as you can, because we're not only talking about time, we're talking about flow. You need to write quickly to stay on top of the flow. You don't want to get bogged down in your first draft.

I personally believe that you have to write for more than an hour a day to get into the groove. The first hour is really just a warm up for what follows in the hours after. It may not seem like it during the first hour, but once you're going into your third hour, you're in the flow and you can just crank it out.

Writing first drafts for nonfiction is a different process than writing first drafts for fiction. For one thing, in nonfiction, the burden of making up fantastical things is absent; and for another, the organization is usually more apparent in the material itself—in the steps of the program, the historical timeline of the events, or the flow from main point to main point. With nonfiction, you're dealing in specific information. It's all about organizing that information in a way that the reader can best use and access it. This particular technique I learned from James Roche, a marketing expert known as "The Info Product Guy" (www.infoproductguy.com).

To begin with, you're going to need some tools. First, you'll need a flip chart, which is usually made of huge, white sheets of paper. Second, you're going to want to get some Post-It notes. It would be great if you could get someone to coach you through this because you'll want another set of eyes and another source of suggestions. The idea is to take this paper and put it up all around your office, using one sheet for each chapter and writing the chapter titles at the top of each one.

Then, using the Post-It notes, you're going to create content for these chapters. What you're looking to do here is to break this up so that each chapter is going to have approximately six main topics, each with five sub-points. Ideally, you're looking to fill in those Post-It notes with the points for each topic. Then, as you're standing among the pieces of paper all around the room, just brainstorm for ideas on how these chapters can be filled.

It's great to have someone coaching you because it helps to have somebody else saying, "Wow! Let's try this" or "Oh, let's try this." You just fill up the pages a lot faster when you work as a team.

Of course, to fill up the Post-It notes, you have to think about what you want to say. For instance, if you have a chapter on sales, then maybe you're going to want to break that up into six particular topics that would include maybe cold calling, direct mailing, and online sales, etc. For each topic, you want to make points. For cold calling you might want to talk about the quality of voice, quality of the contact list, and what time these calls should be made. Point for point enhancement is really what you're going to put under each topic, and that's how you're going to fill the sheet.

Remember, the first draft is just a brain dump. Its purpose is just to get the ideas up on the wall so you have something to work with when you get to the organizing phase. Once you have everything on the wall filled in, you're going to want to look at each sheet and go through all of the ideas on it, really nailing them down into sections. Remember, each big sheet is a chapter, within which the main points are expressed, the stories chosen, and the exercises are listed.

Now, you're making sure that you have clear main topics, specific points you want to make about each topic, and an orderly framework into which to allocate the various points, stories, and steps.

Okay, now this is the fun part. You're going to get a recorder of some sort, a CD recorder, an mp3 recorder, or a tape recorder. Then, you're going to sit down and record yourself talking through everything on your walls. Talk about it as though you're being interviewed, giving about two minutes per point. You'll than have a completely spoken draft of your book in about two to three days. Then, you take that recording and send it out to be transcribed. You could even use voice recognition software on your computer (Dragon Naturally Speaking is one high-quality option) that will create the transcript as you speak. However you do it, with the transcription you automatically have a written rough draft. Then all you have to do is edit and enhance the transcription when it comes back.

Finally, don't forget to enjoy the process. This book is your chance to feel energy flow freely and allow creativity to drive you on. A lot of people get stressed out about putting words to paper, but it doesn't have to be that way. Truly have fun with your creativity and gain satisfaction from putting something out there in the world.

One very important thing you need to do is keep the book real. It has to be something you can hold and touch. As often as possible, print out your first draft pages, especially when you're into the three-hundred-page range. I like to make space in my office to lay the book on the floor in rows, chapter by chapter. If I have twenty-four chapters, I'll have four rows of six chapters all on the floor, so I can get a sense of how it's coming along. I can easily see where some chapters may be longer than the others. I know another writer who hangs his pages on a clothesline in order to get a sense of the book's flow. Whatever you decide to do, make sure you get physical sense of how the book is taking shape.

Once my book is all around me on the floor, I go through it and make notes. I will take a Post-It note from the flip-chart sheet and say, "Okay, in this chapter this is what's happening, in this chapter this is what's happening" and stick those notes on top of each chapter on the floor so that I can look over the notes at a glance and see the flow of the book.

In addition, when my chapters are laid out on the floor, I can tell just by picking them up whether they seem heavier or lighter than the others. I can say, "Okay this chapter feels really heavy; is this too long? Why is this chapter so long?" You may not notice that on the computer because the computer just scrolls down and before you know it, you've scrolled through twenty-five pages. But if it's in print, and you're picking it up and holding it you'll say, "Okay, let me look at what's in this chapter," and you'll sit down and thumb through it. It makes you more aware of what you're doing with the book and how you're pacing it.

If you are a perfectionist and you have that little editor on your shoulder, kick him off! Do whatever it takes to get that little voice out of your head for a while. There's a place for him, and he can come back and help you perfect it once you have that draft out. But that little guy can keep you from getting a draft done in the first place.

If You Really Can't Do This on Your Own...

DON'T!

If you really want to be totally hands off, you can even hire a ghostwriter to do the editing and enhancing of that transcription. That happens a lot, more than people realize. With a lot of nonfiction books, the author is not the person who sat down and wrote the book.

I spent fifteen years at Time, Inc., working for *Time* and *People* magazines. As writers we were trained to write from correspondents' material. A bunch of correspondents in the field would report on a story and send in all this material; we would be responsible for turning it into a coherent, 120-line story. Being so proficient at working with other people's material, *People* magazine writers were always being asked to be ghostwriters for celebrity books.

Ghostwriters are actually not all that hard to find. You can go online and do a search, you can ask your agent, or you can ask an editor. Another resource for ghostwriters is Elance.com. People there bid on freelance jobs. You can post your project and the price that you're interested in paying, and people will bid on your project. You can get some very reasonably priced writers that way. You know you're getting good writers because the people who are bidding for your jobs have writing samples posted. You can see how good they are right away, or if they even do projects that are similar to what you want to do. It's all right there.

If you would like my staff at The Done For You Writing & Publishing Company help create your manuscript, we'd be happy to consider your project. Just go to our Web site, www.DoneForYouWriting. com, and read the descriptions of our programs as well as the testimonials of our past clients to see if this process is right for you. You can also call toll free, 866-834-3942.

That concludes our section on the Book Building Circle! I hope all you will use this structure to create some really powerful books that will inform, educate, and—in the best of all possible worlds—change for the better the way we live.

CHAPTER 12

WHAT COMES NEXT:
WHEN YOUR BOOK BECOMES YOUR BUSINESS

"The time I spent with Sophfronia and the other participants during the program was both educational and motivational. The materials provided are a gift that just keeps on giving. They have helped to move me forward in writing my professional blog, my business plan, my children's book projects, and all my other writing projects. Both sides of my business—my publishing business and my freelance paralegal business—have exploded. Thank you, Sophfronia!"

Ramona Reynolds
Reynolds Work Inc. | British Columbia, Canada

Once your book is published you'll find that many more ideas and opportunities related to the book will come to you. This is when **your book *becomes* your business**. Jack Canfield has done really well at doing this. The system you've created is almost like a movie and merchandising. As a Mel Brooks character says in the film *Spaceballs,* "Merchandising! That's where the real money from the movie is made!"

At a very basic level, you can take the system you teach in the book and turn it into high-fee workshops or keynote speeches. It can become a series of products—or even a series of books when you apply the same system to different situations. Take *The E-Myth* by Michael Gerber, for instance: not only is the E-Myth a whole coaching program, it's also a line of books for managers, medical professionals, and different types of companies. If you look at the material closely, it's not all that different. It's just been repackaged.

Why You Can Re-Purpose Your Material Again and Again

Some people might be concerned that if the material is in the book, no one will come to a workshop or pay to come see them speak. But when someone connects to the material, he or she usually wants more, even if it's just to see you in person. Don't be afraid to re-purpose your material over and over again. If you need confidence, just look at how the big guys have been doing this for ages!

Think about every popular book series you know. The *Rich Dad, Poor Dad* books all have different titles and different foci, but the material is pretty much the same. Dan Kennedy has masterfully been re-packaging his material for decades. The information in his book, *No B.S. Wealth Attraction for Entrepreneurs* is also taught in a weekend seminar. That seminar has been recorded and sold on its own as a CD set. The wealth attraction information also shows up in his *Renegade Millionaire* products.

Are there people who buy one thing and not the others? Of course. But there are also *many* people who buy each and every one of these offerings. That's a lot of money Mr. Kennedy would have left on the table if he had not created and sold the other products and services.

Here are some formats to consider. All or none may suit your purposes, but you get the idea—your book can be so much more. Just use your imagination and go for it!

Audio Programs

Here's the beauty of an audio program, whether it be a CD or a down-loaded mp3 file: while it may be easier to produce than an entire book, it is seen as having a higher value than a book—isn't that interesting? People are impressed by seeing your photo on a CD cover because there's still a mystery to the general public about how they're made. But more and more small studios exist, as well as computer technology to help you create recordings all on your own.

Another benefit of audio recordings is that they help people relate to you as a real person. They get to hear your voice and connect to you. They also hear your authority and your command of your material.

You can also go to sites such as www.PolylineCorp.com to produce your own covers for your CDs. I've done this myself and it's pretty simple. You just slip the image behind the vinyl sleeve on the packaging and you're ready to go.

Your audio program can be a stand-alone product or it can be included in the materials you use for workshops or teleseminars. The program can be included in the price, or you can make it a pre-requisite that your students must purchase it before the workshop.

Re-Purposing Alert

An audio program doesn't have to be something recorded in a studio. You can record any speaking engagement or workshop that you're already doing and turn that into a whole four-, six-, or eight-CD set of material. You can create a workbook for the package by printing copies of your PowerPoint presentation or any handouts you may have used, and binding them. FYI, a workbook can boost the price of your audio program by thirty to fifty dollars.

Make Sure It All Looks Good

I know guys like Dan Kennedy like to teach the idea of *just get the product out there, it doesn't have to be pretty.* And that may work if you do most of your sales over the Internet. After all, the person searching for information on the Internet is more interested in the information, not how it looks.

But if you're selling the product in person, it's another matter. Many of the buyers at your in-person events will be buying on impulse, and they won't be attracted to a product with tacky production values and graphics that look like you drew them yourself. You want to send the message that you are truly professional and your materials are exactly the same. You can accomplish this by having a graphic designer create the cover and back page for your product. (I use www.KillerCovers.com.) You can also get stock photos from www.iStockPhoto.com or www.clipart.com.

Videos and DVDs

In the same way you can make audio recording of your talks to create product, you can do video recordings as well. I know of several business owners who give high priced workshops, record the audio and video of the proceedings, and then sell the "workshop in a box" version of the event for a price that's not as high as the live event but still a high price on its own. They can do that because DVDs have a higher perceived value that CDs or books—you're moving right up the media ladder!

This also boosts your credibility because your customers will get to see the faces of the people you're helping. Many speakers even record video testimonials from the attendees and include them in the product.

(You have to make sure the attendees sign a video/audio release allowing you to record their voice and image. Don't assume all people will be willing. You'd be surprised by how many decide to not sign, and then you have to edit them out of everything.)

Re-Purposing Alert

Video is popping up on many Web pages these days. Have you noticed how some of the teachers from *The Secret* have clips of their appearances on *Larry King Live* on the first page of their sites? I've seen other business owners use clips from appearances on the local news or a television show.

I recommend that anyone who speaks, even if it's not professionally, have at least one video made of their work. At the very least, you can use it as part of your speaker's kit to help you get future engagements. So many places ask for them these days that it's only natural to have it on hand. You also won't need to have the whole event on tape, just a clip for your kit. Keep that in mind if you can't afford to reproduce an entire video. With that in mind...

Keeping an Eye on the Costs

The rise of YouTube may have you thinking otherwise, but it really is difficult to produce a quality video on your own. Producing a video is expensive, especially when you factor in the costs of editing and duplicating. You'll also have to hire a cameraman and maybe even rent equipment (lights and camera) to do the actual recording. And, unlike audio, you can't cost effectively duplicate videos one-by-one. That means if you decide to go the video route, you have to make sure that you're charging enough to make back your investment.

Workbooks

Your first question might be "how is a workbook different from the book I've already written/or am writing?" Never underestimate the fact that people want more. Many authors follow up popular how-to books with workbooks that allow readers to apply the method to their particular project. *Writing the Breakout Novel* was followed by the *Writing the Breakout Novel Workbook*. Likewise *The Marshall Plan for Novel Writing* was followed by *The Marshall Plan Workbook*.

This is where your proprietary system comes into play. A good workbook should teach the skills featured in your proprietary system. It will make clear how the reader will benefit from the system and give him or her plenty of space, examples and suggestions to work through it.

Coaching Programs

Your material will lend itself to the coaching format if it has a motivational aspect to it. For instance many marketing experts teach and coach around marketing, but mindset is so important that clients often want the ongoing support of the marketing expert they're learning from.

Ideally people will buy a fixed number of sessions for a fixed amount of time. They can work with written materials such as your workbook or perhaps a special manual you create just for the coaching program. Of course, you can price any type of customization accordingly.

Teleseminars

Teleseminars are group conference calls conducted over a conference bridge line where hundreds of people can meet and hear the same speaker at the same time. It's kind of like a classroom on the phone. The speaker can mute all listeners to cut down on noise, then open up the call for questions after the presentation is over. I conduct several workshops in a teleseminar format. I've also done many more teleseminars as individual, stand-alone products and to promote larger, move expensive products or retreat programs. Sometimes I'll have a guest interview me or have past clients on the call to give testimonials. These guests help validate the value of what is being offered and can tell how it has helped them.

I also like that teleseminars are easy to set up. These days you can get free bridge lines and recording services on sites such as www.freeconference.com or www.basementventures.com. Most people can fit one into their schedules and you can provide recordings (for free or for a fee) for those who can't make it. There's also the advantage that you're available to anyone in the world who has long distance service on their telephone. I've had listeners from as far away as Spain and Australia on my calls.

Speaking/Keynote

In your speeches you'll be delivering a taste of your proprietary system, but not everything. Especially when you're a keynote speaker, your goal is more to ignite the audience with just the idea or concept of your material. I recently heard a keynote address by speaker/author/marketing expert Joe Vitale where he spoke about being bold and taking unconventional chances with your marketing.

He explained WHAT bold, unconventional marketing was all about. He also gave many examples from his own experience. He talked about WHY it would be beneficial for one to think in this way. But he did not explain HOW to do it. The idea is if you want Mr. Vitales' particular assistance in doing what what he outlines, you might want to hire him to help you. Now he didn't say that directly, but his material was so engaging, as was he, that it felt like a natural next step. Indeed he was approached by many afterward and I'm sure there were prospects for him in the group.

Public Seminars

Many great speakers have made their names in public seminars, but it's not an easy road. Developing, marketing, filling, and conducting public seminars is very hard work—and it's expensive. You have to rent a large venue, publicize the event, and charge enough to cover your costs. But people like Peter Lowe seemed to have cracked the formula. Lowe's Success Seminars used big names such as Ronald Reagan, Norman Schwarzkopf, and Zig Ziglar to fill seats. The money in public seminars is made both from the price of admission and from selling products in the back of the room. Ideally you have the chance to upsell attendees to more expensive products and programs as well. You'll build your customer list undoubtedly, but beware: someone attending a free or low-priced seminar will not be as loyal or highly qualified as someone who responds to an ad or buys an expensive product from you upfront.

Workshops/Boot Camps

If you've done a good job of developing your proprietary system, there's no reason it can't translate really well into a 2 or 3 day workshop or boot camp. A workshop or boot camp can be a great moneymaker since you can charge as much as $5,000 for each attendee. Here's how these things work. Note that you don't have to do all the presenting/heavy lifting yourself and you won't want to—it's too hard to hold up that kind of energy for 3 days!

You are the featured star. So the bulk (but not all) of the talking will be done by you. You might speak for part of each day. The rest of the time you participate in panel discussions, hot seats, and perhaps the interviewing of other experts. Consider it your party and you are the "host."

Include lower level experts. When you're not doing the talking, you'll have other speakers who present on a topic related to the subject of the event. I recently attended a weekend on sales strategies that also featured speakers on public relations, writing sales letters, and sales design.

Include hot seat presentations with audience members. People love this. You basically choose people at random and then spend thirty minutes or so dissecting their particular situation and then work with them using your methods.

Provide prep materials, including a workbook. This should include handouts from each speaker as well as space for taking notes.

Printed Newsletters with Paid Subscribers

Despite the rising costs of printing and postage, printed newsletters are a huge industry and more popular than ever. Why? Because they generate a more qualified list of subscribers that are more dedicated to you, the provider of all this great information. Subscribers might follow your advice in all that you write about, whether it's business activities, investment advice, or how to stay healthy. Dr. Andrew Weill has a wellness newsletter that costs more than a magazine to subscribe to. That's nothing to sneeze at!

If you go this route, make sure you create a high-quality publication with information that makes your reader feel they are getting exclusive, insider information. The better your newsletter, the more you can charge. Many newsletter subscriptions cost as much as one hundred to two hundred dollars a year because the readers see the information as worth so much more.

Joint Ventures

Don't feel your prospects are limited to the people on your own lists. Other companies with whom you don't directly compete may have customers who would be great prospects for you as well. A joint venture agreement would let you leverage these customers, as well as the time, money, and expertise that company has already spent to build up a database.

How I Will Broaden my Business

Choose the ways you would like to re-purpose your book material and how you plan to produce it or make it happen. Remember, be imaginative—you don't have to be limited by the options presented here.

You know your business better than anyone else. But I encourage you to think big and make the commitment to follow through and implement your ideas. You're really stepping out in a major way here—make every moment and every idea count!

The Last Word

By now I hope I've passed onto to you some of my energy, passion, and confidence in what a book can do for your business. But you might be wondering how I came to have such emotion for the medium. **You see, I take books seriously because I know the power of books.**

My father, rest his soul, never learned how to read. He lived with a really limited view of the world. He saw limited opportunities, limited possibilities. My view would have been the same if it hadn't been for books. Books showed me there was much more to the world.

In a book that I had as a child I read about Helen Keller and her desire to attend Harvard. I aspired to do the same, and I did. Then I took my Harvard education and became a successful magazine journalist, writing and editing at *Time* and *People* magazines. But my career and life changed again for the better and when was that?

When I published my first book!

To me, books are no joke. I don't play around when it comes to putting words on paper in a way that can help and influence millions of people. That's why I only create programs that will get the best results—and the best book—out of you! I want for you to learn how to fit writing into your business every day so that you're not just creating one book, you're writing book after book just like T. Herv Eker, Donald Trump, or Jack Canfield.

You won't know how much of a difference you can make until you begin. So get started! And if you need assistance in the endeavor, it's here. Good luck and good publishing!

Bonus Materials

Bonus Chapter

TRADITIONAL PUBLISHING: OF AGENTS AND BOOK PROPOSALS

When it comes to publishing nonfiction with a traditional publishing house, a lot of entrepreneurs get confused about how much does and doesn't have to be done before they approach editors and agents. They also have questions about what to do first. If this is you, then you'll want to get the bonus chapter that didn't make it into this book for space reasons. It's a meaty discussion of all the steps involved in getting an agent, writing book proposal, and attracting a publishing house. You can get it at our Web site:

www.doneforyouwriting.com/bonuschapter.htm

Bonus Marketing Plan

A marketing plan outlines your complete strategy for what you'll do to bring attention to your book. In terms of your book project, it is really the third leg of a three-legged stool. Writing and publishing are the other two. You've spent some time and effort getting your book written and published, but if you don't market your book, how will anyone know it's out there? It would also be difficult for you to take advantage of the benefits that come from being a published author if you don't market your book.

You may download the **Author Marketing Plan** that we use with our clients, including our exclusive **Author Marketing Calendar**, by going to

www.doneforyouwriting.com/bookmarketingplan.htm

You'll find that if you diligently use the plan and calendar, marketing your book will be a much easier process.

The Done For You Writing & Publishing Company Programs

"Working with Done For You Writing and Publishing is everything that I've been looking for in the last five years but hadn't been able to find. The ease of the process is unbelievable. In just a few weeks of working together, I had an amazing manuscript in my hands, one that was exactly the vision of what I had in mind. The process was effortless and so authentic, and I'm so excited to be able to reach out to so many more people as a result of having this book. I am excited to become an even bigger marketing expert in the marketplace, beyond my already loyal base of five thousand subscribers. I anticipate getting many more solo entrepreneurs to become members of my Client Attraction programs and even more paid speaking gigs, which will more than easily cover the already reasonable fee that Done For You charged. If you have been waiting too long to write your own book, put yourself in the capable hands of Done For You. Like me, you'll be wishing you'd done it years before!"

Fabienne Fredrickson

Client Attraction Mentor, author, speaker, information marketer and creator of "The Client Attraction System(TM) | www.ClientAttraction.com

You have five different options to choose from, depending on the type of book you want to produce, how much help you'll require in putting it together, and based on your budget level:

The Done For You VIP Total Access Mentorship and Publishing Program

- **Two Days of In-Person Work in which we:**

1. **Assemble/Organize Your Materials**
2. **Clarify Your Message for Your Book**
3. **Target Your Audience**
4. **Develop Your Process**
5. **Create Your Outline and Table of Contents**
6. **Interview and Record You Talking through Your Book**

(You are responsible for your writer/editor's travel and workspace expenses.)

- **Complete Manuscript Creation**
- **Complete Book Production**
- **Professional Editing**
- **Professional Cover Design and Text Layout**
- **ISBN Assigned to Your Book**
- **Complete Book Distribution**
- **Custom Marketing Plan**
- **500 Finished Copies of Your Book**

This VIP Program is for busy speakers and entrepreneurs who have accumulated a library of material from their past work but need help in figuring out how to turn it all into a book. They also prefer to work in person since they are time crunched and want to be able to devote a couple of days solely to the project so they know it's properly delegated and off their plate.

The Get Published Now Program

- **3-4 Phone Sessions with Your Writer/Editor in which we:**

1. **Create Your Outline and Table of Contents**
2. **Interview and Record You Talking through Your Book**

- **Complete Manuscript Creation**

- **Complete Book Production**

- **Professional Editing**

- **Professional Cover Design and Text Layout**

- **ISBN Assigned to Your Book**

- **Complete Book Distribution**

- **500 Finished Copies of Your Book**

The Get Published Now Program is for high-achieving individuals who are already clear on what they want their book to be about and have done a good amount of content organization on their own.

The Write Now Program

- **3-4 Phone Sessions with Your Writer/Editor in which we:**

1. **Create Your Outline and Table of Contents**
2. **Interview and Record You Talking Through Your Book**

- **Complete Manuscript Creation**

The Write Now Program is for individuals who only need a manuscript written because they already have other plans to get the book published.

The Quick E-Books Program

Creation of an E-Book, (80 page limit)

- **1-2 Phone Sessions with Your Writer/Editor in which we:**

1. **Create Your Outline and Table of Contents**
2. **Interview and Record You Talking Through Your Book**

- **Complete Manuscript Creation**

The Quick E-Books Program is for speakers and entrepreneurs looking to quickly create an easy, downloadable product to sell or give away on their Web site.

Workshops and Seminars

Business Book Bootcamp

This twelve-week strategic planning program is for entrepreneurs who want to know how to plan their book up front to get the results they want. During the bootcamp we will show you how to set up your book for **effective lead generation**, **customer attraction,** and the creation of future **products**, **workshops,** and other business **opportunities**. We will also coach you on how to finish writing your own book.

Go to www.BusinessBookBootcamp.com to register for our next session.

To learn more about these programs and to see if your project is right for our company, please call toll free 866-834-3942 or go to our Web site at www.DoneForYouWriting.com.

Books for Your Reading List

This list represents a range of books. Some of them are great examples of books used as lead generation tools. Some are books that I consider important reading for entrepreneurs who are preparing to step into the spotlight. I believe that if you're going to write, you must read. If you're going to read, find the best stuff out there and don't be afraid to learn from it. Your book will help someone else when you decide to publish. This is one of the unspoken benefits of authorship: you get to take the good energy and pay it forward!

The 4-Hour Workweek: Escape 9-5, Live Anywhere, and Join the New Rich
By Timothy Ferriss

Make It BIG!: 49 Secrets For Building a Life of Extreme Success
By Frank McKinney

No B.S. Wealth Attraction for Entrepreneurs
By Dan Kennedy

No B.S. Time Management for Entrepreneurs
By Dan Kennedy

The Ultimate Marketing Plan
By Dan Kennedy

Brilliance Unbridled
By Kendall Summerhawk

The Success Principles: How to Get from Where You Are to Where You Want to Be
By Jack Canfield

The Tipping Point
By Malcolm Gladwell

Instant Income: Strategies That Bring in the Cash for Small Businesses, Innovative Employees, and Occasional Entrepreneurs
By Janet Switzer

Jeffrey Gitomer's Little Black Book of Connections: 6.5 Assets for Networking Your Way to Rich Relationships
By Jeffrey Gitomer

Winning Through Intimidation
By Robert J. Ringer

A Plentiful Harvest: Creating Balance and Harmony Through the Seven Living Virtues
By Terrie Williams

See You at the Top
By Zig Ziglar

Secrets of Closing the Sale
By Zig Ziglar

The Joy of Doing Things Badly: A Girl's Guide to Love, Life and Foolish Bravery
By Veronica Chambers

How to Meet the Rich
By Ginie Sayles

Secrets of the Millionaire Mind
By T. Harv Eker

The E-Myth Revisited
By Michael E. Gerber

Power and Soul
Compiled by Alexandria K. Brown

The Secret
By Rhonda Byrne

The Writings of Florence Scovel Shinn
By Florence Scovel Shinn

The War of Art: Break Through the Blocks and Win Your Inner Creative Battles
By Steven Pressfield

The Elements of Style
By Strunk & White

Attitude is Everything: 10 Life-Changing Steps to Turning Attitude into Action
By Keith Harrell

If Success is a Game, These Are the Rules: Ten Rules for a Fulfilling Life
By Cherie Carter-Scott, Ph.D.

Bonus Articles

by Sophfronia Scott

HOW TO REALLY FINISH YOUR BOOK

I have finishing on the brain these days. I just finished a large project with another close to completion. I'm also working on urging clients to finish reviewing and editing their own manuscripts so they can move on to the publishing process. But I reached a new level of thinking about this while listening to a recording of performance coach Lee Milteer where she talked about finishing. A friend of hers had been working on a book for several years, but he passed away before finishing it.

"Why does that happen?" I wondered. Why do some people finish books and others don't? I began to look closely at my own process and what I observed in others. I considered all sorts of projects large and small–because I believe our thinking is similar no matter what the size. Here's what I learned. I hope these tips will help you finish.

What Happens When You've Finished?

When I look at what things motivate the most, I noticed the big dream was pretty enticing: the vision of leaving a legacy, wanting to communicate to a bigger audience, wanting to have a presence in the world as an author. All these are nice goals, but they're missing one thing: they're not immediate. Think about it. When you had to pull an all-nighter in college to finish a paper, were you thinking about the overall message of the paper? No! You just knew you had to finish it or get a poor grade! There was an immediacy to the situation!

I finished my project recently because it was part of a bigger picture—and I couldn't proceed until I had finished this part of the picture. With a deadline approaching, there was an immediacy I couldn't ignore.

Now, think about your book. What will happen when you're done with it? Do you really have plans for your book, or will it be a "Wow, I finally did it, that's great and that's all" kind of thing? I'm willing to bet just completing the book will not be enough for you. How can you make your situation immediate so you *must* finish?

What Happens If You Don't Finish?

Of course there must be consequences of your not finishing. Will your business not grow? Will you lose money? How will you feel? Really focus on this. If you don't have a consequence big enough to motivate you, create one! Make a deal with a friend, so you have accountability, that if you don't finish your book you will do something that would be absolutely horrifying for you. Maybe it's making a donation to an organization you dislike, or giving away a favorite gadget or keepsake.

How Will You Feel If You Don't Finish?

Once you figure out that consequence, I want you to really connect with the feeling of that consequence. How uncomfortable will you really be? A little or a lot? Does it really matter to you, or is it discomfort you think you can live with? After all, life has its disappointments, right? It's that kind of thinking that will sabotage you when you least expect it!

Is What You're Feeling Enough to Get You to Finish?

If what you're feeling isn't bad enough to make you finish, then you'll have to come up with a different consequence. If that doesn't work, find another one. If that doesn't work, you may have to be honest with yourself and decide whether writing a book is truly important to you. It's okay if it isn't. Just because writing a book means something to a lot of people doesn't mean it must hold the same importance to you. In fact, coming to the realization that it isn't your thing will free up your time, emotions, and energy to pursue a goal more in line with who you are. And I'll be the first to say, "Go for it!"

BOOK MARKETING:
WHEN THE STATS DON'T APPLY TO YOU

Americans are reading less. That's the conclusion of a recent study by the National Endowment for the Arts. It's a follow up to an NEA survey that found an increasing number of adult Americans were not even reading one book a year. This information can be depressing, especially if you've been spending all your precious time writing a book. Are you creating something that no one will ever read? Not necessarily. If you have crafted your book and planned your marketing properly,

these statistics will NOT apply to you!

Here's why. The majority of the public doesn't read. But the majority of the public is not your audience! Think in terms of the 80/20 rule: 20 percent of a group will most likely provide 80 percent of your business. Your job is to make sure you're targeting—and finding—your people, your 20 percent.

Who Is Your Target Reader?

Some writers have trouble thinking in terms of "audience" because it seems like a vast, faceless mass. So instead thinking of your target audience, think of your target reader–one person. This can be someone real or someone you've idealized in your mind. When I was writing my first novel, I had one of my co-workers at *People* magazine be my first line reader because I felt she embodied my target market. When I wrote, I kept her in mind as though I were sitting in her office telling her the story word for word.

When you think of your reader, ask yourself many questions. How old is this person? Are they male or female? Where do they live? Where do they work? Are they married or single? With children or without? Do they live in the city, country or suburbs? Where do they shop? What kinds of activities do they pursue? The clearer you can be, the easier it will be for you to bring this person to mind. You can even give them a name—maybe you're writing for an Audrey, a Matthew, or a Chandra.

Where Will You Find Them?

Once you know your target reader, where can you find them so you can put your book in front of them? Remember, it doesn't have to be the usual channels. If you've written a book on wellness and nutrition, your book doesn't have to be in a Borders or a Barnes & Noble to find your reader. It might be easier to find them in a yoga studio or a health food store. If you write for entrepreneurs, you could find them in a Staples, an Office Max, or in airport bookstores. You can do joint ventures with other authors or entrepreneurs who have lists full or your ideal readers. Be creative here. The only limit is your imagination.

Don't Forget International Markets

Remember, the NEA study only covered the United States, which means there can be many, many readers waiting for you all over the world. If your book is sold on the Internet, your book is available everywhere. You can also use webinars, chatrooms, and blogs to make your book tour a globetrotting event, all from the comfort of your home.

Keep in mind that sales and audiences have dropped in many areas and industries: television, movies, houses, cars, baked goods. Does that mean they stop making these items entirely? No! They just know they have to do things differently. The same goes in the book world. Go find the different way that works for you.

THE RISE OF SELF-PUBLISHING

Our local newspaper recently featured an area Realtor on the cover of its magazine supplement. It was a large story including a photo of the woman on the top of the newspaper's front page teasing the story and referring to her as a book author.

I was curious to know more about her book so I checked it out. As it turned out, the Realtor had published the book herself, and it wasn't her original idea–she had bought the license to the subject (how to sell your house in a tough environment) and tailored it to the area of the country she represents. But did that matter? No! The paper treated it as though it were any book that might have been published by a big New York City publishing house. And if you asked any of her readers if they knew the difference, I'm willing to bet they wouldn't know because the information on how to sell their house was what they wanted, not who published the book!

Not long ago, self-published books were considered just a few steps above pamphlets run off on a Xerox machine. How did this big change come about? Let's look at a few points:

Quality Product

The amazing changes in printing technology have made it possible for self-published books to be produced with a level of quality that can rival that of books done by traditional publishers. In the past the look and feel of a self-published book was the telltale sign that it wasn't a "normal" book. The design (of both text and cover) was often poor and the paper sometimes badly cut. These days, print on demand companies can offer similar, if not the same, technology used by traditional publishers—and they can do it without requiring print runs of thousands of copies that often ended up unsold in authors' garages and basements. And many of the designers used by traditional publishers also freelance their services out to self-publishers. Again, the same quality and talent is available that was once only accessible to the big companies.

When I sought out a company to partner with for my **"Get Published Now"** program, I chose **Advantage Media Group** specifically because of the quality of their final product. I wanted to be able to deliver a good-looking finished book into the hands of my clients. You should want the same for yourself.

The same goes for editing help. Many self-publishing companies offer editing as part of their packages. It's also easier to find a professional editor for hire via sites such as Elance.com. You can ensure that your book reads well and is free of typos and continuity problems.

Respectability for Being Published–No Matter the Form

Many newspapers and magazines didn't review self-published books, and there are some that still don't. But now they look at it this way: a good story is a good story. If your book handles a subject that's important to their readers or viewers (like the real estate example above) or hits upon a trend currently in the news, the media will be very interested in doing a story on you and your book. Again, it won't matter how it was published. On television they seldom mention the publisher, and in print they note the price and publisher no matter how large or small the company.

Distribution Problems Gone

Once upon a time, bookstores resisted stocking self-published books. Why? Because unsold books are usually returned to the publisher and the store doesn't have to pay for them. But unsold self-published books were non-returnable, which made them more of a risk. However, many companies, including Author House and Advantage Media, have made it possible to include distribution as part of their publishing services. That means they have worked out deals where self-published books can be returned, making it easy for you to have your book available in stores. Note: a store may still choose not to stock your book, but if someone comes in and asks for it, your book can be ordered by the store. If they get enough of such requests, they may decide to stock it after all.

Affordability

While quality self-publishing is still an issue of "you get what you pay for," you don't have to spend what you used to in order to get your book done well. Many companies package their services in ways that allow you to pick and choose what you want in the production process.

The Choice Is Yours

Is self-publishing right for you? Only you can know for certain. Consider all the things you want out of being published—what will a book do for you or your business? Is this book just for you and your family, or is it for the masses? Do you have a way of getting the book's message out to the public? How will you sell it? The best way for you to be satisfied by the publishing process is for you to be clear about what you want and then pursue the path that will get you there. Self-publishing might even be the shortcut you're looking for.

HOW TO CULTIVATE A GOOD HABIT

It happens every year and still it takes me by surprise—the conclusion of the Tour de France. I wake up the morning after and feel the distinct void of having no reason to turn on the television. I'm always amazed at how watching the Tour quickly becomes a part of my life, so much so that it's a shock when I stop doing it.

I realize now that it all happens because I cultivated the habit of watching the Tour using the same tools that I use year after year. But this year it finally hit me that I could use the same tools to cultivate any new good habit that I want to bring into my life. You can do the same, whether you want to cultivate an exercise routine or a reading regimen. Let's look at the very simple components of this habit-forming system and how you can customize it for yourself.

Consistency

Simply put, you have to do something every day for it to become a habit. I watched the Tour de France every single day it was on. I even viewed the rest day programs so I could stay connected with any news coming down the pike (and in this Tour there was a lot!). So that's the first step for your habit: **build consistency**. Maybe every day is too much for what you want to do. Start with a specific day. You could make Tuesdays your yoga day or your reading day or your rest day. But do it every Tuesday for at least two months to get the feeling it will stick. You want to get to the point where you'll know you miss it if you don't do it, just as I could tell from the moment I woke up that the day was different because the Tour was over. I missed it.

Support

It's easier to maintain a habit when others are helping you do it. My husband would watch some of the finishes with me or stop our son Tain if he was trying to put a DVD into the TV during a crucial part of a stage! I recently presided over a Writers Challenge week for my workshop students where the members had to write as much as they could in a given week. But before the challenge began, they had the assignment to tell their family what they would be doing and discuss what help they would need to be productive for the time. How can your family help to support your new habit?

Automatic Reminders

Sometimes it's hard to keep up with a habit all on your own. Setting up automatic reminders can help. If I couldn't watch the Tour de France during the day, I always had little reminders that made sure I tuned in at night. I received e-mails from Active.com and subscribed to a blog by one of the writers covering the Tour so that I could stay plugged in even when I was busy. During our Writers Challenge the students had to report in to the group on how they did that day. Getting the e-mails from everyone else served as the automatic reminders that helped each student keep his or her head in the game. Perhaps a reminder for you could be subscribing to a series of motivational e-mails, or a regular check-in with a friend who's supporting you in your new habit.

No Struggle

Remember this above all: cultivating your habit should feel natural and easy. Don't make yourself feel like you're handcuffed to a ball and chain. If the new habit feels like too much of a struggle, re-think it. I don't think twice about committing the time each July to the Tour. It's just something I do, and it's easy and fun. Of course, one could argue that it's easy and fun because I only do it for one month. If it were any longer it might be a different story! But I don't believe that–witness the attention lavished on baseball and basketball; those seasons go way longer than one month! But if a habit is important enough to you the time won't matter and you will be the winner in the long run. Just start small and take it one day at a time.

ANTHOLOGIES: YOUR SHORTCUT TO GETTING PUBLISHED

What do you get when you mix a handful of writers, a hot topic, and a snazzy title? You get an **anthology**—and one of the more popular form of books being published today. A recent article in the Sunday *New York Times* noted that "the wave of anthologies has not yet crested" and the phenomenon is still a great seller, especially for women writers.

You can take advantage of this trend to get yourself published faster than working on your own. I know it might not be what you dreamed, sharing a byline and being in a book that's not wholly yours, but it is a way for a first time author to get a foot in the door—and I know of at least one publishing company, **Love Your Life Publishing**, with a program designed to help you do it in as little as six months! (You can find them at www.loveyourlife.com. Tell them The Book Sistah sent you so they'll treat you *really* well!) Here's how you can start the legwork on your own.

Choose Your Topic

Anthologies are organized and driven by their subject matter, and the title usually makes it crystal clear what that subject is. Examples: *Maybe Baby: 28 Writers Tell the Truth About Skepticism, Infertility, Baby Lust, Childlessness, Ambivalence, and How They Made the Biggest Decision of Their Lives*; *The Bastard on the Couch: 27 Men Try Really Hard to Explain Their Feelings About Love, Loss, Fatherhood, and Freedom*. When you choose your topic you'll want it, of course, to be something you're interested in writing about, but you'll also want it to feel as though you are responding to what's on the minds of a particular group or society at large. You'll want to do your best to plug into the zeitgeist because that's what will generate buzz about your book and get you interviewed in the media.

Gang Up! Find Your Co-Authors

Next, find other writers interested in participating. You can do this by Googling your subject and seeing what writers are already working in the field. You can also scan online groups, like on Yahoo, to find unpublished writers looking to do their first book as well. Note, if you are not self-publishing, you may need to entice a few known authors onto your list in order to pique a traditional publisher's interest.

FYI, Love Your Life Publishing is looking for contributors to an anthology they're assembling entitled *The Spirit of Women Entrepreneurs*. If this is your expertise, contact Love Your Life for more details.

How Will You Publish and Split Costs?

If you self-publish your anthology, you'll have to come up with a plan for how you'll handle the costs and oversee the project. Will it by "your baby," in which case you'll pay for the book's production (and possibly even pay the bigger name writers if that's what it takes to get them involved) and marketing costs? If you go in with a group of first timers, you'll all be able to split the costs, but it might be a good idea to have someone act as the project manager to keep from having a "too many cooks" scenario develop.

Co-Market for Your Best Results

The best part about working with more than one writer is that you'll be able to use the muscle of marketing to more than one list. Ideally each writer will have his or her own list (either personal contacts or a list developed as part of a business) and that automatically multiplies the number of people you can reach with the book. You'll want to put your heads together to develop a good marketing plan so you're all sending out similar materials with a similar message.

Again, you can designate a project manager to handle submitting the book to media markets (your co-authors can handle local media if they already have their own contacts). Hopefully everyone will pitch in and do their share. After all, if the book succeeds, it could be the stepping-stone the writers need to their own individual book contracts!

WHAT BRUCE SPRINGSTEEN TAUGHT ME ABOUT WRITING

The year 2005 marked the thirtieth anniversary of the release of Bruce Springsteen's groundbreaking album *Born to Run*. Columbia Records celebrated by re-releasing the disc with lots of audio and video goodies including interview material of Bruce discussing the writing of this seminal work. I'm a fan, so you can imagine I was gobbling up the stuff like Thanksgiving had come early!

What hit home for me was hearing about how Springsteen's back was really up against the wall while he was creating this album. His record label was considering dropping him, so he knew he had to make something happen. When people ask me, "How do I know if my work is good enough?" I think of Springsteen because surely he wasn't asking that when he was trying to figure out what to write. The answer could have been "it's not" if he had asked someone at his record company. He had to work and learn for himself how to tell if his work was good enough. This is what I learned from how he did it.

1.) Learn From the Great Ones

In the summer of 1974 Springsteen could have been lamenting the fact that his first two albums had not been successful and he was living in a tiny house in New Jersey while the country was in the throes of a severe economic depression. But he wasn't. He was focused on his songwriting. "I had a record player by the side of my bed," he wrote in his book, *Songs*. "At night I'd lie back and listen to records by Roy Orbison, the Ronettes, the Beach Boys, and the other great sixties artists. These were records whose full depth I'd missed the first time around. But now I was appreciating their craft and power." Notice he wasn't saying, "There's no way I can create songs like that!" Instead he was considering, "What can I add to the conversation?" He was getting inspired and educated at the same time.

2.) Aspire to Be Great Yourself

In an interview about *Born to Run*, Springsteen says he knew his record company was about to drop him. He added, "I knew I had to write something great." But he didn't *have* to write something great. He could have folded up his tent and said, "They don't like me, so I'm just gonna stay in Asbury Park and play where people appreciate me and that's it." But he didn't do that. He also didn't ask whether he was good enough. He simply challenged himself to go beyond himself–to be great. Ask yourself: what are you writing right now, and is it challenging you to be great? What would it take for you to start thinking this way?

3.) Find Trusted Ears for Feedback

Yes, it is hard to know on your own whether you're on track with your writing. That's when you recruit your own inner circle of readers whose ears and eyes you trust. Jon Landau became one of those trusted pairs of ears for Springsteen. They became friends during the writing of *Born to Run*, and Bruce often sent Jon, then a Boston music critic, tapes of the work as it progressed. When the work stalled, Jon was the one who came in and helped Bruce put it all together. Who can be those ears or eyes for you? Try to keep the inner circle small. If you have too many opinions showered on your work it may cloud your creative judgment.

4.) Try Something Different

Most of the songs on *Born to Run* were written on piano–this from a guy known for his raucous Fender guitar. But writing on piano gave Springsteen new ideas and presented new opportunities for him to explore. It also gave the album an amazingly emotional and intimate vibe that I find intoxicating. What can you do differently that can inspire a leap to your next level? Set your novel in 1905 instead of 2005? Write from the point of view of the opposite sex? Be a little creative with your nonfiction? Take a chance. No effort is ever wasted even if you're writing badly–you can still learn from what you've done wrong.

5.) Think Local, Write Global

One of the changes Springsteen made with *Born to Run* was that the characters in his songs were "less eccentric and less local" than the ones on his previous albums. The people in *Born to Run* "could have been anybody and everybody," he says. "When the screen door slams on 'Thunder Road,' you're not necessarily on the Jersey Shore anymore. You could be anywhere in America." And it's true. Millions of people connected with–and bought–*Born to Run*. I sought the same kind of connection for my novel. Though the family in *All I Need to Get By* is African-American, I've had readers of all races tell me how they have seen themselves in one or more of the characters and how they related strongly to the book's family issues. Touching people in this way is key to developing an attentive audience. How can you open up your work to a larger audience while still being true to your story?

If you still have doubts, think of this quote from Ralph Waldo Emerson: "Whatever course you decide upon, there is always someone to tell you that you are wrong. There are always difficulties arising that tempt you to believe that your critics are right. To map out a course of action and follow it to an end requires...courage." Be courageous for yourself and your writing. Your own *Born to Run* may be waiting to come out.

Printed in the USA
CPSIA information can be obtained
at www.ICGtesting.com
JSHW062328060224
56783JS00027B/781